# CONDITIONALS

# Conditionals

MICHAEL WOODS

*Edited by*
DAVID WIGGINS

*with a*
*Commentary*
*by*
DOROTHY EDGINGTON

CLARENDON PRESS · OXFORD
1997

Oxford University Press, Great Clarendon Street, Oxford OX2 6DP
Oxford New York
Athens Auckland Bangkok Bogota Bombay
Buenos Aires Calcutta Cape Town Dar es Salaam
Delhi Florence Hong Kong Istanbul Karachi
Kuala Lumpur Madras Madrid Melbourne
Mexico City Nairobi Paris Singapore
Taipei Tokyo Toronto
and associated companies in
Berlin Ibadan

Oxford is a trade mark of Oxford University Press

Published in the United States by
Oxford University Press Inc., New York

British Library Cataloguing in Publication Data
Data available

Library of Congress Cataloging in Publication Data
Data available

ISBN 0–19–875126–5 ✓

1 3 5 7 9 10 8 6 4 2

Typeset by Invisible Ink
Printed in Great Britain
on acid-free paper by
Biddles Ltd, Guildford and King's Lynn

# EDITOR'S PREFACE

This monograph derives from one chapter of Michael Woods's projected book *Philosophical Logic*, a full-length, comprehensive, and self-contained work which the Oxford University Press was to have received in January 1994. Michael Woods fell ill in the Autumn of 1992 and died on 2 April 1993. The material that the author left at his death was transcribed and placed in order by his Brasenose colleague, John Foster. In the end it appeared to publishers and executors that the only continuous section that did not present intractable problems was Chapter 9, the treatment of conditionals. In advance of their arranging for anything else to be attempted, they asked me to edit this for publication. This section was both complete and self-contained. Indeed, Woods had read extracts from it at various meetings.

As the reader will swiftly appreciate, the aspirations of this fragment transcend altogether those of any textbook treatment of the kind that the author was contemplating for the range of questions that he had chosen for his treatise in philosophical grammar. What we have here, albeit without the many revisions, amplifications, finishing touches, and emphases its author would have inserted, is an original essay on one of the oldest, most troublesome questions of logic.

The essay contained a beginning, middle, and end and a continuous development, but it lacked many things the philosophical public now expects. Turning at the outset for help with various bibliographical questions to Dorothy Edgington, my then colleague in the Philosophy Department at Birkbeck College and an authority within English-speaking philosophy on the subject of conditionals, and enlisting her further help in supplying certain extra materials that the author had indicated his settled intention to include, I was drawn to the idea that my colleague might be willing to furnish a commentary on Woods's essay. This would bring the essay to the attention of a wider public and push the argument about certain of Woods's crucial contentions yet further, all in a way that I believe he would greatly have welcomed. The result of her co-operation is a book that advances these long-standing inquiries with appreciably increased staying power.

In addition to thanking Dorothy Edgington most warmly for undertaking her commentary, I would draw attention to the magnitude of John Foster's contribution. This included a prolonged struggle with problems of transcription from multiple versions on the author's obsolete word-processing system, not only of Chapter 9 but also—in advance of the publishers' and executors' detailed deliberations—of the material from all the other chapters.

Pending the publication of any other works, I take the opportunity to include in this volume a bibliography of Michael Woods's published writings (a model of quality and restraint to hold up to our troubled times, and a pointer in the direction of the important and larger things which he was making careful preparations to complete in due time). I also reprint John Ackrill's memoir.

I shall end this Preface with a personal statement. I first met Michael Woods in 1953–4 when we were both undergraduates (reading Literae Humaniores, that is, Latin, Greek, ancient history, and modern and ancient philosophy) at Brasenose College, Oxford. Each of us was eagerly interested in philosophy, but I think he took to it much more quickly and single-mindedly than I did. Indeed, despite the fact that he was in the year after me, I think he *found* himself in philosophy years before I did.

After 1955, when I went down, Michael and I did not meet for three or four years, because he stayed at Oxford to do the B.Phil. In this period, 1955–8, while I was engaged elsewhere in other (mostly non-philosophical) things, he wrote a marvellously good thesis about Aristotle on predication and individuation ('Substance and Quality'). He was elected to a Harmsworth Scholarship at Merton, and was then appointed a lecturer at Christ Church. In October 1959, when—one week late and a hundred times less well prepared to fulfil the role than Michael was—I came back to Oxford from the USA to a teaching post in philosophy at New College, we met again and we graduated from acquaintances to friends. Among many other kindnesses, he lent me a copy of the said thesis.[1] He gave me at short notice reading

---

[1] Twenty years later, but before his death, having made reference to it in a book of mine about identity, I tried to give my copy of the thesis to the Bodleian. When I told Michael that I would do this, he did not forbid it, but nor did he

lists for essays and other bibliographies. He told me the kinds of thing I needed to know if I was to survive in my new role. When I had want of this, he also helped me to understand better what Aristotle says about this or that (an office in which he continued well beyond emergency). We gave together some cheerful and (at least for us) very amusing university seminars (as well as many joint revision classes, in the sixties for Brasenose and New College undergraduates, and in the eighties for Brasenose, University College, and other undergraduates). The first of these university seminars, which was given in 1961–2, and the very last, which was given in 1985–6 with Michael Ayers, were about identity and individuation.

If you had asked me in any of the four decades in which I knew him what Michael Woods was like, I should have said the same as I should say now. First, he was clever and acute to a degree that was invisible to the stupider students (and even to colleagues sometimes) if they were fooled by his extreme hesitance or his good manners. He had good philosophical judgement and flawless philosophical taste. As a translator he made smooth accurate versions which (in defiance of all vagaries of fashion) were also literate and readable. (To look into these versions now is to perceive the distance between the condition of the chapter that we publish here with editorial repairs, insertions, and other first aid and the chapter that he would himself have published.) In the second place, Michael was a tireless and wicked gossip, chiefly distinguished among that class of persons by his preference for probable stories in which colleagues and others could be seen as having acted not merely in character but more than merely in character. Thirdly, in friendship, as in all other kinds of personal relations, he was truly generous. That is to say that he was generous with things that mattered. His benevolence towards me in 1959 was typical of him. To help to edit one of his last works is for me a consoling but inadequate act of reciprocity.

*New College, Oxford*                                  David Wiggins
*April 1996*

encourage it. (I say 'tried' because, disastrously, it got mislaid en route to the Manuscript Collection. I hope someone else has a copy.)

# CONTENTS

# CONDITIONALS

# I

# The Varieties of Conditional

Conditional statements appear to involve a form of sentence composition, but one that is non-truth-functional (that is, the truth-value of the conditional sentence appears not always to be determined by the truth-values of its parts). However, whether these appearances are correct is, for a number of reasons, rather hard to determine. One thing that gives rise to doubts about the truth-functionality of conditional statements is that it seems so easy to construct sentences which have no natural use but which would have to be counted as expressing truths if conditionals are understood truth-functionally. In fact, though, our intuitions about the truth-values of such utterances are far from clear. We are not ready with an answer to the question what the truth-value is of such a bizarre conditional as

'If Rome is the capital of Greece, there are no snakes in Ireland'.

As we shall see, we *can* envisage a special context in which such a conditional would be asserted; but normally the utterance of that conditional strikes us as simply bizarre.

Further, the question whether conditional utterances always, or even ever, have a truth-value is itself open to dispute. In the first place, although attention has generally been concentrated upon utterances of the conditional form used to make assertions, such as

'If it rains this afternoon, the match will be cancelled',

we also find conditional clauses occurring in sentences of the imperative and interrogative forms. If there are conditional assertions, there are also conditional commands and conditional questions. Consider the following examples:

'If James has resigned, who has replaced him?'

'If James has resigned, did he do so voluntarily?'

'If you were born before 1 April 1963, please tick this box.'

'If you walk about this town after dark, keep to the main streets.'

In citing these examples, I have been assuming that the 'If'-clause functions in a similar way. In what follows, I shall concentrate upon assertions, and consider non-assertoric conditionals separately in Section 7.

Within the class of assertoric conditionals, it has been customary to distinguish two kinds by marking off what have been variously called 'subjunctive' or 'counterfactual' conditionals. According to an established tradition, the following would be counted as non-counterfactual:

(1) If it rains this afternoon, the match will be cancelled.

(2) If Jones was present at the meeting, he voted for the proposal.

(3) If Oswald did not assassinate President Kennedy, someone else did.

(4) If he caught the train, he will arrive on time.

(5) If this animal is an antelope, it is a ruminant.

Contrast with these

(1′) If it rained/were to rain this afternoon, the match would be cancelled.

(2′) If Jones were/had been present at the meeting, he would vote/would have voted for the motion.

(3′) If Oswald had not assassinated President Kennedy, someone else would have.

(4′) If he had caught the train, he would have arrived on time.

(5′) If this animal were/had been an antelope, it would be/would have been a ruminant.

All of these would, according to the tradition, be classified as subjunctive or counterfactual conditionals.

It has commonly been recognized that neither 'subjunctive' nor 'counterfactual' is happily chosen. The subjunctive exists at best only vestigially in English;[1] but many writers continue to use the label, on the assumption that those conditionals that have traditionally been described as subjunctive do exhibit a recognizable grammatical or syntactic form. In practice, the conditionals regularly thus classified are those containing 'would' in the main clause and a past tense in the 'if'-clause.

'Counterfactual' may seem to be less open to objection. What lies behind this piece of terminology is not, of course, that the antecedent is in fact false, but that, in some way, the falsehood of the antecedent is implied, whether the conditional is true or false, well supported or not. Thus, we should normally expect

'If Hitler had invaded England in 1940, he would have won the war'

to be uttered by someone who knows that Hitler did not invade England in 1940 (and did not win the war). But when the question is raised exactly *how* the falsehood of the antecedent is implied by the conditionals, problems arise.

It seems reasonably clear that it would be misguided to regard it as a matter of *entailment*. If we consider the case of someone who utters the conditional,

'If Jones had come to the party, there would have been a row,'

believing wrongly that Jones did not come, they might be reluctant to continue to utter the conditional when they know that Jones *did* come; none the less, the speaker's discovery that he was wrong in supposing the antecedent to be false would hardly be regarded as requiring the admission that what he had said was false. But it has commonly been held that *some* implication is

---

[1] See V. H. Dudman, 'Indicative and Subjunctive', *Analysis*, 48 (1988), 113–22, for criticism of the use of the label 'subjunctive conditional'. (In some conditionals of the relevant sort, we do find the subjunctive 'were', for instance, 'If he were here, he would be very surprised' or 'If you were to buy us all a drink, your popularity would rise'. But it is by no means clear that all the conditionals philosophers have classified as 'subjunctive conditional' are properly so called.)

carried by the form of words used in conditionals commonly cited as counterfactuals that the antecedent is false.[2]

Formulating the view more precisely, it might be said that there is a conventional or semantic implication carried by such features as the tense or mood of the verb that the speaker believes that the antecedent is false; and this has commonly been taken as defining the broad class of counterfactuals.

In fact there is no class of conditionals that convey that the speaker believes the antecedent to be false in virtue of their verbal form alone. Any conditional which, in one context, may appear to carry such an implication will not do so in another. Where such an implication *is* carried, it is pragmatic in character, generated by the semantic properties of the sentence that require to be explained in some different way, *in conjunction with features of the context*.

Thus someone who says,

'If the allegations had been true, he would have denied them,'

may well *not* be conveying any belief that the allegations are not true. Again, someone may say,

'If that bird were a canary, it would be yellow,'

in the course of arguing that the bird in question *is* a canary. Yet in these cases, we have the form of words that has been held to be distinctive of a counterfactual conditional.

What is certainly true is that conditionals that involve these forms of words are typically used—are especially apt for use—in circumstances in which it is known that the antecedent is not, or will not be, fulfilled. Any theory must therefore allow for this.[3]

---

[2] Thus Mackie (*Truth, Probability, and Paradox* (Oxford, 1973), 65) writes:

'"If he had come he would have enjoyed himself" differs from the corresponding open conditional "If he came he enjoyed himself" only in suggesting, fairly strongly, that he did not come and, less strongly, that he did not enjoy himself';

and again (p. 71), he writes:

'It is not [the antecedent's and consequent's] falsity in fact that puts a "counterfactual conditional" into this special class, but the user's expressing, in the form of words he uses, his belief that the antecedent is false.'

[3] Since that is so, we should expect that, in some cases where it is not common knowledge that this is so, the use of the form of words will generate a pragmatic

The upshot of all this is not only that counterfactual or subjunctive conditionals are not aptly so named, but that it is not possible to define the required class in the way in which it has traditionally been defined.[4] Nevertheless it is still generally assumed that there are two broad classes to be distinguished. As has been recognized, what would count as strong, or conclusive, support for a non-counterfactual conditional would not support the corresponding counterfactual.[5] Thus from the truth of

Someone assassinated J. F. Kennedy

the truth seems to follow of

'If Oswald did not assassinate J. F. Kennedy, someone else did.'

But it seems clear that those same grounds would not support

'If Oswald had not assassinated J. F. Kennedy, someone else would have.'

Again, to take an example used by F. P. Ramsey much earlier,

(1) Everyone present at the meeting voted for the proposal

---

implication of the falsehood of the antecedent. It is interesting to note that something parallel may be said about paradigmatically *non*-counterfactual conditionals. As we shall see, such conditionals are typically used when the speaker is ignorant of the truth-value of the antecedent, and thus a pragmatic implication may be generated in some contexts that the speaker is thus agnostic; but any such conditional which, in one context, generates such an implication, may be used in another in which the speaker displays his knowledge, or belief, that the antecedent is true. (Consider someone who says, 'If he missed the train from London, as he certainly did, he missed the connection at Didcot.')

[4] It was recognized by Alan Ross Anderson in 1951 ('A Note on Subjunctive and Counterfactual Conditionals', *Analysis*, 12 (1951), 35–8) that conditionals traditionally classified as counterfactual do not imply the falsehood of their antecedents; but it was some time before this came to be generally recognized, as we saw from Mackie's 1973 article in *Truth, Probability, and Paradox*. (At about the same time, David Lewis wrote that ' the counterfactual constructions of English do carry some sort of presupposition that the antecedent is false. It is some sort of mistake to use them unless the speaker does take the antecedent to be false, and some sort of mishap to use them when the speaker wrongly takes the antecedent to be false': *Counterfactuals* (Oxford, 1973), 3.)

[5] This way of putting the point gives the impression that it makes sense to speak of the counterfactual *corresponding to* an open conditional. For present purposes, and to avoid anticipating later discussion, I confine the explanatory task to the description of the examples cited.

conclusively supports (entails, surely)

> (2) If Jones was present at the meeting, he voted for the proposal,

but it does not support

> (3) If Jones had been present at the meeting, he would have voted for the proposal.

Given appropriate beliefs about Jones's voting intentions, someone who accepted (1) might consistently decline to accept (3), but they could hardly reject (2); in fact, they may use it to infer, in conjunction with their knowledge of Jones's voting intentions, that he was not present.[6]

Faced with a considerable diversity in conditional statements, and with an apparent broad division into two classes, theorists have responded in a variety of ways. Some theorists have offered quite different accounts of the two broad classes; others, mindful of the implausibility of supposing that 'if' works in radically different ways in the two types of case, have offered a broadly uniform treatment of conditionals, and included within that general theory an explanation of when the counterfactual form of words is appropriate, recognizing that it is not simply a matter of a speaker's belief in the falsehood of the antecedent.

Although the term 'counterfactual' is ill-chosen, it will be convenient to use it in scare quotes of those conditionals which have been regularly so classified in the literature, leaving it open, for the time being, whether others belong to the same class.

---

[6] See F. P. Ramsey, 'General Propositions and Causality', in *The Foundations of Mathematics* (London, 1931), 249. The phenomenon just mentioned, that counterfactual and non-counterfactual conditionals are differently supported, is already sufficient to show that the habitual method of distinguishing them by the implication of the antecedent's falsehood hardly touches on what is central to counterfactuals. If it were true that

> (1) If it rained yesterday afternoon, the match was cancelled

differed from

> (2) If it had rained yesterday afternoon, the match would have been cancelled

only in implying the falsehood of its antecedent, then the difference in the way in which they were supported would be unexplained. This is clear from the fact that it is possible, as things are, for a speaker to add a rider to the effect that he believes the antecedent to be false without altering the character of the evidence required to ground the conditional.

If we assume that the meaning of 'if' is constant in

(1) If Oswald did not assassinate Kennedy, someone else did

and

(2) If Oswald had not assassinated Kennedy, someone else would have,

then one thing that distinguishes them would seem to be that in (1), we have two sentences, each capable of being used to make an assertion on its own, combined by a certain construction—the 'If . . . then . . .' construction; whereas in (2), the main clause is not a sentence that could be used on its own to make an assertion. The words in the 'if'-clause form a sentence that *could* be so used; but it would then say that Kennedy was assassinated at some time previous to a time itself past relative to the time of the utterance. But the words, when they occur in the 'if'-clause, clearly do not express, as a hypothesis, an occurrence of something thus doubly past: they do not express, as a hypothesis, what would be asserted by those words used on their own.[7]

This is apparent from the fact that such forms of words can occur inside an 'if'-clause with an explicit present or future time indication.

'If he had come now, he would have been very surprised'

and

'If he had come next Tuesday, he would have been very surprised'

are readily intelligible, but 'He had come next Tuesday', uttered on its own, is not.[8]

If I am right in holding that *some* conditionals—roughly, those that have traditionally been classified as 'indicative'—are

---

[7] This is a point stressed by Dudman, 'Indicative and Subjunctive'; see also Jonathan Bennett, 'Farewell to the Phlogiston Theory of Conditionals', *Mind*, 97 (1988), 509–27.

[8] That, in the case of 'counterfactuals' , we do not have, in the 'if'-clause, a sentence expressing, as a hypothesis, what that same sentence might have asserted to be the case, uttered on its own, is very clearly apparent from those 'counterfactuals' which have (if any do) the subjunctive in their 'if'-clause, as in 'If he were here, he would be very surprised'.

adequately described as involving an application of 'If . . . then . . .' to a pair of sentences, we should expect that a general account of 'If . . . then . . .' will be available which explains the meaning of an arbitrary sentence of this form (its assertibility-conditions and truth-conditions, if any) as resulting from the general meaning of 'If' interacting with the meaning of the particular sentences filling the gaps. I shall refer to those sentences in which we simply have an application of 'If . . . then . . .' to a pair of sentences as Simple Conditionals. For the reasons given, we should not regard 'counterfactual' conditional sentences as simply resulting from the application of 'If . . . then . . .' to a pair of sentences. The distinctive syntactic features of 'counterfactual' conditional sentences are found elsewhere; most obviously in the past tense (even if that tense does not work in the same way inside an 'if'-clause as it does elsewhere), but also in expressions like 'would' and 'would have'. Compare 'I thought she would come' and 'In 1932, he would have been under twelve years old'. So it is natural to look for an explanation of the meaning of 'counterfactual' conditionals given in terms of the general meaning of 'If . . . then . . .', as found in Simple Conditionals, and the semantic properties of the past tense and of 'would', etc., as found elsewhere.

Accordingly, I will start with Simple Conditionals, and consider how 'If . . . then . . .' should be understood, taking as examples what seem to be clear and uncontroversial cases of an application of 'If . . . then . . .' to a pair of sentences each of which could be used on its own.

# 2

# Theories of Simple Conditionals

If the truth-value (or possibly the absence of truth-value) of Simple Conditionals is fixed solely by the truth-values of their antecedents and consequents, there seem to be only two possibilities. First, if we take the view that 'If . . . then . . .' sentences *always* have a truth-value, there is, in fact, no alternative to treating them as material conditionals, if they are truth-functional. This is a consequence of the fact that 'If P and Q, then Q' is always true, whatever the truth-values of P and Q are, and that not all 'If . . . then . . .' statements are true. 'P and Q' cannot be true if Q is false, but the other combinations of truth-value assignments to P and 'P and Q' are not ruled out.[1]

If, on the other hand, truth-value gaps arise, it seems reasonable to hold that they lack a truth-value when the antecedent is false, and, if the antecedent is true, they are true or false according as the consequent is true or false. Thus we envisage the following truth-table:

| If | P, | then | Q |
|---|---|---|---|
| | T | T | T |
| | T | F | F |
| | F | N | T |
| | F | N | F |

---

[1] Cf. Dorothy Edgington, 'Do Conditionals Have Truth Conditions?', *Crítica*, 18 (1986), 7, reprinted in Frank Jackson (ed.), *Conditionals* (Oxford, 1991), 179–80. The argument is as follows. Suppose (a) a conditional always has a truth-value which is a function of the truth-values of its parts; and (b) that (*) 'If P & Q, then P' is always true, whatever the truth-values of P and of Q. (i) Let P and Q be true. Then (*) has a true antecedent and consequent, and is (*ex hypothesi*) true. So any conditional with a true antecedent and consequent is true. (ii) Let P be true and Q be false. Then (*) has a false antecedent and true consequent, and is (*ex hypothesi*) true. So any conditional with a false antecendent and true consequent is true. (iii) Let P be false. Then (*) has a false antecedent and false consequent and is (*ex hypothesi*) true. So any conditional with a false antecedent and consequent is true. (iv) We have established three out of the four lines of the truth-

where 'T' and 'F' respectively signify truth and falsity, and 'N' signifies the lack of a truth-value.

If, however, we treat Simple Conditionals as material conditionals, so far as truth-conditions are concerned, we are forced to recognize, as we saw in the last section, that many true conditionals could not be uttered non-misleadingly outside a special context. Following a recent tradition, we can say that many natural language conditionals, if interpreted as material conditionals, though true, would not be *assertible*.[2] Accordingly, we can speak of their *assertibility-conditions*. One thing that commands general agreement is that the *assertibility-conditions* of natural language conditionals do not coincide with the *truth-conditions* of the corresponding material conditionals.

It is a characteristic of assertions in general that something may be true but not (non-misleadingly) assertible—for example, if asserted without grounds, or again if the person making the assertion does not believe it to be true. But these are *general* conditions for the assertibility of a proposition, and derivable in a straightforward way from its truth-conditions. With conditionals, there seems to be a divergence of quite a different sort between truth and assertibility, if they are taken as material conditionals; someone may believe that a material conditional is true, and have adequate grounds for that belief, in circumstances in which the corresponding natural language conditional would not be assertible.

It may be suggested that, rather than speaking of the assertibility-conditions of a conditional, it would have been better to speak of its *acceptability* conditions. It might be thought that to treat assertibility-conditions as central directs attention too much upon the phenomena of public utterance, whereas an adequate

---

table for conditionals, given assumptions (a) and (b). The fourth case (unrealizable by (\*)), is the case of true antecedent and false consequent. If the conditional were true in this case, it would be true for *all* combinations of truth-values of its parts: all conditionals would be tautologies. Adding the assumption (c) that not all 'If . . . then . . .' statements are true, we have shown that if conditionals are truth-functional, the standard truth table is the only possibility.

[2] The tradition begins with H. P. Grice. See his William James Lectures, in *Studies in the Way of Words* (Cambridge, Mass., 1989). A more recent version is due to Frank Jackson, 'On Assertion and Indicative Conditionals', *Philosophical Review*, 88 (1979), 565–89; 'Conditionals and Possibilia', *Proceedings of the Aristotelian Society*, 81 (1980–1), 125–37; and *Conditionals* (Oxford, 1987).

theory of conditionals is centrally a theory about when they are accepted and rejected—whether or not they are true or false—and what the grounds are for accepting and rejecting them. Further, it may be thought that assertion is tied to utterances that can be assessed as true or false; whereas the truth-valuedness of conditionals is problematic, as already mentioned.

But clearly there must be *some* description of what someone does who utters

'If Jones was at the meeting, he voted for the proposal'

as a serious utterance, in normal circumstances, that contrasts it with a conditional command or conditional question, examples of which were given in Section 1; if it cannot be classified as an assertion in a strict sense, there must be a wider sense of 'assertion' in which that sentence counts as one, even if it lacks a truth-value, and 'assertibility' can be understood correspondingly. It is preferable to present the issue in terms of assertibility-conditions, because the phenomena that a theory of conditionals is directly answerable to are those of actual use. Presumably, the assertibility-conditions of conditionals will, in their turn, determine the conditions in which they are accepted.

It is clear, then, that it must be one of the tasks of the theorist of conditionals to state clearly in what their assertibility-conditions consist. Theorists have responded to the mismatch between the assertibility-conditions of natural language conditionals and the corresponding material conditionals in a variety of ways.

(i) Some have held that, despite appearances, natural language conditionals are equivalent in meaning and in truth-conditions to material conditionals. Such a position, which has a long history, needs to be supplemented with an explanation of the divergence between truth-conditions and assertibility-conditions in terms of pragmatic considerations. Such a view has been most recently proposed by Grice, who tried to explain the phenomena of natural language (simple) conditionals employing general principles governing conversational interchange.

(ii) Alternatively, it may be held that natural language conditionals and material conditionals have the same truth-conditions but differ in meaning. Such a view may recommend itself if the attempt fails to explain the phenomena pragmatically. Such a position has been taken by Frank Jackson and, recently, by David

Lewis.[3] There is room for a diversity of explanations of what the difference in meaning is between 'If . . . then . . .' and the material conditional '⊃'.

(iii) Some have held, as mentioned earlier, that 'If P then Q' is true if P and Q are both true, and false if P is true and Q is false, but that otherwise it has no truth-value.[4] This view has been held to be a consequence of regarding an utterance of 'If P then Q' as a conditional assertion: an assertion is made if P is true, but not otherwise.[5] Such a theory will still need to explain why it counts many conditionals as true that would not ordinarily be asserted (for example, 'If Washington is the capital of the United States, Cairo is in Egypt'), and others as lacking truth-values that are naturally regarded as true or false (for example, 'If Queen Victoria ascended the throne in 1840, she was the first British monarch to do so under the age of twenty').

(iv) However, in view of the counter-intuitive character of many of the ascriptions of truth-value to natural language conditionals that (i), (ii), and (iii) require, it may be suggested that Simple Conditionals are *not* truth-functional: the truth of 'P ⊃ Q' may be held to be a necessary but not a sufficient condition for the truth of 'If P then Q'; some further conditions may be required for the truth of 'If P then Q', and so the denial of 'If P then Q' may be true without the truth of P and the falsehood of Q. Various suggestions have been made about the further condition for the truth of 'If P then Q' beyond the truth of the material conditional. On some versions of this view, 'If P then Q' has been analysed as an assertion *about* the propositions expressed by P and Q—the assertion that Q follows from P, together with certain other assumptions to be gathered from the context. It is thus treated as a *metalinguistic* assertion.

---

[3] Jackson, 'On Assertion and Indicative Conditionals', 'Conditionals and Possibilia', and *Conditionals*; Lewis, postscript to 'Probabilities of Conditionals, and Conditional Probabilities', in his *Philosophical Papers*, ii (New York, 1986), 152–6.

[4] W. V. O. Quine suggests this in *Methods of Logic*, 3rd edn. (London, 1974), 19.

[5] von Wright has adopted this position; Dummett, without accepting it, regards it as the position that must be taken by anyone who elucidates Simple Conditionals by means of the notion of conditional assertion. See G. H. von Wright, *Logical Studies* (London, 1957), 131; Michael Dummett, 'Truth', *Proceedings of the Aristotelian Society*, 59 (1958–9), 141–62, reprinted in his *Truth and Other Enigmas* (London, 1978), 1–24, at 10–11.

(v) Finally, in response to the difficulties in specifying a proposition stronger than the material conditional that is expressed by 'If P then Q', a number of writers have held that Simple Conditionals lack truth-values; they have held that the task of describing the way in which such conditionals are used has been completed when their assertibility-conditions have been specified. Such a position has been taken by Ernest Adams, Allan Gibbard, and others.[6] The denial that Simple Conditionals are truth-valued is sometimes accompanied by the claim that 'If P then Q' is to be regarded as a condensed argument from P to Q (early Mackie, Dudman), or as an assertion of Q within the supposition that P (later Mackie). This may be seen as a variant of the position that 'If P then Q' is a conditional assertion (of Q). (That is how conditionals are regarded by Ernest Adams.)

Our immediate concern is with Simple Conditionals, and most of the theories just described are put forward to account for them. It is generally recognized that the truth of 'If P had been the case, Q would have been the case' requires more than the truth of the material conditional 'P ⊃ Q'; and utterances of 'counterfactuals' are not plausibly thought of as conditional assertions. But the type of theory described under (iv) may offer an account of the truth-conditions of Simple Conditionals using a theoretical framework devised for 'counterfactuals'. This is true of a metalinguistic theory such as those of Chisholm or Goodman, as well as of theories such as Stalnaker's, which introduce a possible-worlds framework.[7]

At first sight, it is a condition for the truth of 'If P then Q' that there be some *connection* between the antecedent and the consequent.

> 'If Washington is the capital of the United States, Cairo is in Egypt'

is bizarre, it seems, because there is no connection between what is expressed by the antecedent and the consequent. The relevant

---

    [6] Ernest Adams, *The Logic of Conditionals* (Dordrecht, 1975); Allan Gibbard, 'Two Recent Theories of Conditionals', in W. L. Harper, R. Stalnaker, and G. Pearce (eds.), *Ifs* (Dordrecht, 1981), 211–47.
    [7] R. Chisholm, 'The Contrary-to-Fact Conditional', *Mind*, 55 (1946), 289–307; Nelson Goodman, *Fact, Fiction, and Forecast*, 4th edn. (Cambridge, Mass., 1983), ch. 1.

notion of connection requires elucidation; but, even in advance of that, it is clear that many conditionals are asserted in circumstances in which there is no question of any such connection. Suppose that I am asked whether the party was a success if John did not attend it. I may know, independently, that the party was a success, and believe that that was so irrespective of whether John attended or not; in which case I surely must answer 'yes' to the question, even though I evidently hold that the party's success was independent of John's presence, and would thus not wish to claim any connection between antecedent and consequent. In general, when someone believes that Q, whether or not P (and thus believes there is no connection between P and Q), they must accept 'If P then Q', even if it might be misleading to assert it.

Various suggestions have been made to elucidate the notion of connection. For example, according to the Consequentialist Theory, as stated by Mackie, the claim is that in saying 'If P then Q', we are saying that Q is some sort of consequence of P, or 'P would ensure Q'.[8] What is required is a connection between P and Q such that the truth of P would be a ground for the truth of Q, or that Q is inferable from P. This is in fact how Strawson has stated this theory.[9]

However, the connection that is allegedly thus marked by 'If . . . then . . .' does not need to be more than *epistemic*. All that it is plausible to suppose that the 'If . . . then . . .' construction indicates is that P and Q are linked, at least for a particular person, given his state of knowledge. Someone's knowledge may be such that, without knowing the truth-value of P or of Q, he may still know enough to rule out the combination of the truth of P with the falsehood of Q. In that case, he will be in a position to *infer* Q should he learn that P. We may say that for such a person, P and Q are *epistemically linked*; but the link is relative to a par-

---

[8] Mackie, *Truth, Probability, and Paradox*, 83.

[9] P. F. Strawson, *Introduction to Logical Theory* (London, 1952), 36. Similarly, L. J. Cohen calls this the 'semantic hypothesis': 'A dictionary entry for the particle "if . . . then . . ." should state that they indicate a connection between antecedent and consequent as well as performing the truth-functional role of ruling out the conjunction of the antecedent's truth with the consequent's falsehood.' 'Some Remarks on Grice's Views about the Logical Particles of Natural Language', in Y. Bar-Hillel (ed.), *The Pragmatics of Natural Languages* (Dordrecht, 1971), 50–68, at 59.

ticular state of knowledge, and is not intrinsic to the circumstances that are the topic of P and Q. For a person thus placed, it will be true that P and Q stand in a ground–consequent relation: the truth of P is, or would be, *in the circumstances*, a ground for the truth of Q.
Relevant examples here are:

'If you try to persuade him, you will find it very difficult'

and

'If the janitor was speaking the truth, no one left the building all night'.

There is no question here of any causal connection between the janitor's veracity and the absence of egress from the building: the conditional in question follows from a simple statement of what the janitor said.

In general, as Grice and others have pointed out, anyone who knows that P and Q are not both true, without knowing which, can naturally and non-deviantly say 'If P then not-Q', no matter how unconnected P and Q are considered in the abstract.[10] It follows that whenever P materially implies Q, 'If P then Q' will be assertible by someone who has evidence of a certain kind for the truth of the material implication. This may be thought to count in favour of a view like (i) or (ii), since it is hard to accept that the truth of 'If P then Q' is relative to a speaker's epistemic state, even if its assertibility is dependent on it.

Since the later 1960s, much work on Simple Conditionals has tended to address directly the task of devising a theory of their assertibility-conditions. Much of this can be seen as a development of an idea found in F. P. Ramsey's classic paper 'General Propositions and Causality'. Ramsey says there:

If two people are arguing 'if P will Q?' and are both in doubt as to P, they are adding P hypothetically to their stock of knowledge and arguing on that basis about Q; so that in a sense 'If P, Q' and 'If P, not-Q' are contradictories. We can say that they are fixing their degrees of belief in Q given P. If P turns out false, these degrees of belief are rendered *void*. If either party believes not-P for certain, the question ceases to mean

---

[10] Grice, William James Lectures, in *Studies in the Way of Words*. See also J. F. Thomson, 'In Defense of ⊃', *Journal of Philosophy*, 87 (1990), 56–70.

anything to him except as a question about what follows from certain laws and hypotheses.[11]

Clearly, such an approach has affinities with those that introduce the notion of supposition in explaining the purport of an utterance of 'If P then Q'. In a typical case, I have no belief about the truth-value of either P or Q. If I add a belief in P hypothetically to my stock of beliefs, I may find that such an envisaged addition carries with it an acceptance of Q, or its rejection. But equally, I may take no attitude to Q's truth.

Ramsey speaks of a *hypothetical* adding of P to one's stock of beliefs, and says that one will accept 'If P then Q' if in those envisaged circumstances, one will accept Q. But if, after hypothetically adding P to one's stock of beliefs, one envisages oneself also accepting Q, the *actual* acquisition of a belief in the truth of P would presumably lead to its acceptance. That suggests two possible accounts of the meaning of Simple Conditionals.

(A) We may think that, in asserting 'If P then Q', I commit myself to Q's being the case, if P is; so Ramsey's view leads naturally to the thought, already mentioned, that Simple Conditionals are used to make conditional assertions; one who utters 'If P then Q' is taken to have asserted Q, in the event of P's being the case. We have a satisfying parallel between conditional assertions and commands.

(B) Alternatively, we may attend to the fact that, if I indicate that a hypothetical acceptance of P carries with it an acceptance of Q, I indicate that, were I to learn that P, I should infer that Q. So it may be thought that 'If P then Q' is assertible when a speaker would be ready to use *modus ponens*, supposing he learned of the truth of the antecedent.

Neither (A) nor (B) excludes the view that Simple Conditionals have truth-conditions, and indeed those of the material conditional. Although Adams and others, as already mentioned, have taken the conditional-assertion view to deny truth-values to conditionals, that follows only if we hold that, if P is false, someone asserting 'If P then Q' makes no assertion at all, not simply no assertion *of Q*.[12] But it is also possible to hold

[11]  Ramsey, *Foundations of Mathematics*, 247.
[12]  Such a position is suggested by an analogy with conditional bets: if the relevant condition is not fulfilled, it is as if no bet had been made.

that a conditional assertion of Q can be made *by* an assertion whose truth-conditions are those of the material conditional. Thus, if we imagine a speech community concerning whom it is stipulated that they use a form of words that is equivalent to the material conditional, it is clear that that form of words would be apt for use to make an assertion of the truth of the consequent conditionally on the truth of the antecedent.

Option (B), which connects the acceptance of Simple Conditionals with a readiness to use *modus ponens*, might seem to coincide with the view, held by some, that the meaning of 'If . . . then . . .' should be explained in terms of its logical powers.[13] But we need to distinguish between the thesis that the meaning of 'If . . . then . . .' is fully explained by saying that *modus ponens* is *valid*—in which case, so are *modus tollens* and the inference from P and Not-Q, to Not-(If P then Q)—and saying that 'If P then Q' is assertible by someone only if they *would accept* Q on learning that P. The first view is essentially the view that Simple Conditionals are fully equivalent to material conditionals. The second thesis claims not merely that *modus ponens* is valid with 'If . . . then . . .' (as it is with material conditionals) but that a Simple Conditional is assertible only when a speaker is ready to use it, which is something more. Though *modus ponens* is valid with the material conditional, someone who asserted such a conditional on the sole ground that its antecedent was false would not be in a position to *use modus ponens*, since the discovery that P was true would undermine the grounds for accepting the conditional. The use of *modus ponens* requires that P and 'If P then Q' be *simultaneously* accepted.

(A) and (B) do not in fact amount to the same position, since (B) says, in effect, that one who can accept 'If P then Q' *will accept* Q on learning that P, whereas (A) says that in asserting 'If P then Q' one *does* accept Q conditionally, the condition being P. There are cases in which the difference is significant. Jackson gives the example,

---

[13] Cf. G. Ryle, ' "If", "So", and "Because" ', in Max Black (ed.), *Philosophical Analysis* (Englewood Cliffs, NJ, 1950), 323–40; R. M. Hare, 'Meaning and Speech Acts', *Philosophical Review*, 79 (1970), 3–24, esp. 16. See also Mackie, *Truth, Probability, and Paradox*, 81.

If Reagan is bald, no one outside his immediate family knows it,

which may be assertible, and is reasonably treated as a conditional assertion, even though a speaker clearly would not wish to assert the consequent in the event of his discovering that the antecedent was true. So (A) and (B) are not equivalent, and the advantage seems to lie with (A).

Ramsey's Test for the acceptability of 'If P then Q'—namely, add P hypothetically to your stock of beliefs and see whether you accept Q—requires both generalization and elucidation. It needs to be generalized to cases in which someone is not wholly agnostic about the truth-values of P and Q. When I already accept Q, then, provided that hypothetical addition of P does not conflict with that, there is no problem about the acceptability of 'If P then Q', as we saw earlier with the example of someone who believes Q, whether or not P.

When P is believed to be certainly *false*, however, Ramsey himself suggests an alternative view in the quotation given and elsewhere, when he says

In general we can say with Mill that 'If P then Q' means that Q is inferable from P, that is, of course, from P together with certain facts and laws not stated but in some way indicated by the context.[14]

This is, in effect, the metalinguistic view already mentioned. The problem to be confronted here is precisely that of *which* other assumptions may be legitimately combined with P in inferring Q. But this problem is essentially the same as that which arises if we stay with Ramsey's other explanation of 'If P then Q' in terms of hypothetical acceptance of P, and consider an application of it to a case in which someone believes P to be false. If I add hypothetically to my corpus of beliefs a belief in P, I shall need to make hypothetical revisions not only to my belief that Not-P but also to my other beliefs.

Clearly, there will be alternative ways in which I can envisage revising my beliefs; some may involve an acceptance of Q, others require its rejection. It seems, however, that when we accept 'If P

---

[14] Ramsey, *Foundations of Mathematics*, 247.

then Q', while believing P to be false, we do so because, after hypothetically accepting P, a *minimal* revision to our beliefs would leave us accepting Q. Thus, I may say,

'If Jones is innocent, most of the witnesses were lying,'

believing that Jones is guilty. I accept the conditional because the smallest revision of my beliefs that a hypothetical belief in Jones's innocence would require will compel me to revise my beliefs about the witnesses' veracity; I do not consider more drastic revisions elsewhere in my system of beliefs that will leave my belief in witnesses' veracity untouched, at the cost of postulating radical changes in the legal system, or a radical misremembering on my part of what the witnesses said.

Much recent work on conditionals is devoted to explaining how our corpus of beliefs is revised when we envisage the addition of the truth of the antecedent of a conditional to them, and, in particular, to clarifying the notion of a minimal revision. Although, from an external standpoint, what we do can be described as making hypothetical revisions to our beliefs, someone deciding whether to accept a conditional will take himself to be revising his conception of how the world actually is, since an individual's set of beliefs embodies a (partial) conception of what is actually the case. So, a hypothetical revision of his beliefs, undertaken to accommodate the supposition that the antecedent is true, can be seen as the envisaging of an alternative possible world to the actual, in which the antecedent is true. The question then arises how a particular possible world, among indefinitely many in which the antecedent is true, is selected. This line of thought is what leads to possible-worlds theories of conditionals (Simple and 'counterfactual').

However, as we shall see, the cluster of theories that import possible worlds into the analysis of conditionals embodies a rather different approach to their understanding from that suggested by the most natural development of Ramsey's Test. In the next section, I examine a suggestion about the assertibility-conditions of Simple Conditionals that has won wide acceptance, and can reasonably claim to be an elaboration of Ramsey. In Section 4, I shall consider in the light of this proposal explanations of the meaning of the 'If . . . then . . .' construction and of the truth-conditions of Simple Conditionals. In Section 5, I consider possible-worlds theories.

# 3

# Ramsey's Test and Adams's Hypothesis

Ramsey describes someone deciding whether or not to accept Q, after accepting P, as making minimal revisions in his other beliefs. On what basis is such a hypothetical revision made? In order to answer this question, it will be useful, and more realistic, to take account of the fact that the acceptance or rejection of a belief is not an all-or-nothing matter, and this applies to the acceptance of 'If P then Q'. In so far as someone has any opinion at all on whether or not P is the case, he will assign to P a certain probability. Since an individual's beliefs are systematically related, they involve assignments of probabilities not only to P and Q separately, but also to their joint occurrence. Idealizing a good deal, we may think of an individual's probability-function as assigning values between zero and one to each of a range of exclusive possible states of the world—alternative possible scenarios—which together exhaust the possibilities, so that the probability-assignments add up to 1. We can then distinguish those scenarios in which the antecedent is true and those in which it is not.

Hypothetically adding P to one's stock of beliefs can then be seen as deleting—or (hypothetically) assigning zero probability to—those scenarios that include P's falsehood, and re-assigning probabilities to those that involve its truth so that the ratio between them is preserved, but they add up to one. We can then say that the sum of the probabilities assigned to the scenarios that include the truth of the consequent, Q, is the conditional probability of Q, given P, or Prob(Q/P). This is in line with what Ramsey said, in a passage already cited: 'We can say that they are fixing their degrees of belief in Q given P.'

In line with this, Ernest Adams, in *The Logic of Conditionals*, suggested that we commonly treat the probability of a conditional as consisting in the corresponding conditional probability.[1] It is important to see that the conditional probability of Q given P is not, in general, the same as the probability of the corresponding material conditional; in particular, the former probability is never greater than the latter, and is normally less than it.

The conditional probability of Q given P is the probability of 'P and Q', divided by the probability that P, provided that the probability of P is greater than zero (if P's probability is zero, the conditional probability of Q given P is left undefined). So the probability of Q given P may be low, even though the probability of the material conditional is high; that will be so in cases in which the high probability of the material conditional is due mainly to the high probability of the antecedent's falsehood: 'P ⊃ Q' may be probable because, or largely because, 'not-P' is highly probable. None the less, the probability of 'P and not-Q' may be a large fraction of the probability that P, low though that is. Thus, the probability that it will snow in England in May is low but, low though it is, the probability of its snowing there in May and snow's not falling in Scotland may be very low in proportion to it. Thus

> 'It will snow in England in May ⊃ snow will fall in Scotland,'

and

> 'It will snow in England in May ⊃ snow will not fall in Scotland,'

are both highly probable, given the high probability of the antecedent's falsehood; but the corresponding conditional probability is high in the first case, in comparison with the conditional probability of the second, because the probability of its snowing in England in May and of its snowing in England and snowing in Scotland also are almost equal: the second is hardly less than the first, though both are low.

One of the arguments in favour of Adams's Hypothesis is that

---

[1] Adams, *The Logic of Conditionals*. See also Adams, 'On the Logic of Conditionals', *Inquiry*, 8 (1965), 166–97, and 'Probability and the Logic of Conditionals', in J. Hintikka and P. Suppes (eds.), *Aspects of Inductive Logic* (Amsterdam, 1966), 265–316.

it offers an explanation of the breakdown, under certain conditions, of inferences that would be valid if 'If . . . then . . .' were taken as a material conditional—and would also be valid on some other views, such as one that explains 'If . . . then . . .' in terms of a connection between antecedent and consequent, or one that explains this in terms of a ground-consequent relation between them.[2] Consider the following putative inference forms.

(i) Transitivity: $P \supset Q, Q \supset R \vdash P \supset R$. But consider: 'If Jones was elected, his name was on the ballot paper. If his name was on the ballot paper, Jones was not elected. Therefore, if Jones was elected, he was not elected.' Or again consider: 'If I went swimming yesterday, the swimming pool was open. If the pool was open yesterday, I did not go swimming. Therefore, if I went swimming yesterday, I did not go swimming.'

(ii) Contraposition: $P \supset Q \vdash$ not-$Q \supset$ not-$P$. But consider the following example of Adams's: 'If it rained yesterday, it did not rain very hard; therefore if it rained very hard yesterday it did not rain.'

(iii) Strengthening the antecedent: $P \supset Q \vdash (P \& R) \supset Q$. But consider: 'If Jones stood for election, he was elected; therefore, if he stood and was involved in a personal scandal, he was elected.'

(iv) The equivalence of $P \lor Q$ to not-$P \supset Q$. But consider this example of Adams's: 'Either it rained in Berkeley last year or it snowed; therefore, if it didn't rain, it snowed.'

---

[2] It is important to see that what we are considering is cases in which the premisses are acceptable, but the conclusion is not. Some valid inference-schemata correspond to inferences that, for perfectly intelligible reasons, we are unlikely to make. Thus, we seldom, if ever, make inferences of the form 'P; therefore, either P or Q'. There are pragmatic reasons for this: if we already know that P, we shall not be interested in acquiring the information conveyed by the disjunctive statement. But it is evident that, if P is true, then so is 'Either P or Q', and, in general, someone who accepts that P will regard someone else's remark that either P or Q as acceptable, even if he would be misleading his hearers if he were to assert it himself. The trouble we are concerned with is that some truth-functionally valid inferences involving conditionals seem to break down in a more radical way than that—in that the premiss is acceptable and the conclusion not.

(v) *Modus tollens*: P ⊃ Q, not-Q ⊢ not-P. But consider this example of Jackson's: 'If he doesn't live in Boston, he lives somewhere in New England; he doesn't live anywhere in New England; therefore he lives in Boston.'

Adams showed that, if we take the acceptability of a Simple Conditional to be measured by the associated conditional probability, and the acceptability of a non-conditional proposition to be measured by its probability, then some inferences that are valid with the conditionals read as material implications are not *probabilistically valid*. Adams gave an exact characterization of this notion of probabilistic validity, which coincides with the classical notion of validity for arguments not containing conditionals.[3] Here we will focus on one consequence. Take an argument with a small number of premisses (for present purposes, one or two). If each premiss can have a very high probability or conditional probability, while its conclusion has a very low probability or conditional probability (that is, if an argument can have highly acceptable premisses and a highly unacceptable conclusion), the argument is not probabilistically valid.

This can be seen clearly from (ii). In circumstances in which heavy rain was unlikely, the probability of heavy rain, given that it did rain, may be low; but of course, the probability of no rain on condition that it rained heavily is zero.

Similarly with (i). The probability that the name of anyone who was elected appeared on the ballot paper is near to 1, given the procedures by which elections are conducted; but Jones's chances of election, given that his name appeared, may have been low; and the conditional probability associated with the conclusion must be zero. Similarly with the other example. Likewise, taking (iii), the conditional probability of Jones's having been elected if he stood may be quite different from the conditional probability of his being elected if his standing was followed by a personal scandal (given that the probability of the latter is low anyway).

What, then, about (iv)? The probability of rain or snow may be high, yet the conditional probability of snow in the absence of rain may be very low indeed. In the case of (v), it is obvious that

---

[3] See Edgington's Commentary, p. 111.

the probability of anyone's living in Boston relative to the information that he doesn't live in New England is zero. But do we have here a case in which the relevant probabilities of the premisses can be high and yet the probability of the conclusion low? The problem is that, given the facts of geography, the conditional probability of someone's living somewhere in New England if he doesn't live in Boston can be high only if the probability of his living in New England is high, in which case the second premiss can't be probable. Putting it another way, if it is highly probable that he doesn't live anywhere in New England, it will also be highly probable that if he doesn't live in Boston, he doesn't live anywhere in New England. What this means in this case is that the inference is ruled out because the second premiss undermines the first. Someone may assert at one time the first premiss, and later discover the second is true, but he can accept it only if he abandons a belief in the first. A similar objection does not apply to the other examples: in the case of (i), the two premisses may be simultaneously assertible, when the conclusion is not; and the other inferences are all inferences from a single premiss.

Another similar example of an inference which is probabilistically unsound according to Adams's Hypothesis is one of the form,

'If P or Q, then R; therefore if Q then R.'

Take

'If Smith stood for election or died before the result was declared, he was elected. Therefore, if Smith died before the result was declared, he was elected.'

In such a case, the conditional probability associated with the premiss would seem to be high, assuming that the disjunction in the antecedent's premiss is much more likely to be true in virtue of the truth of its first disjunct than that of its second. But this example poses a problem for Adams's Hypothesis, because the premiss seems not to be assertible even though the relevant conditional probability is high. In general, we hold that it is justifiable to assert 'If P or Q, then R' only if we are prepared to assert 'If P then R' and also 'If Q then R'; and this is out of line with Adams's Hypothesis. This phenomenon is perhaps best explained by the operation of some pragmatic constraints on the use of disjunctions, which extends to the occurrence of disjunctions in the antecedent of a conditional. I return to this problem in Section 6.

Should we, then, accept Adams's Hypothesis as an account of the assertibility-conditions of Simple Conditionals? It must be stressed that the Hypothesis is offered as an account of Simple Conditionals, even though, as we shall see in Section 5, there are parallel breakdowns in the validity of inferences involving 'counterfactuals'. Adams's treatment of Simple Conditionals presupposes that assertibility, in general, reflects a high probability assignment; exactly how high a degree of probability is required will, no doubt, be relative to the features of the particular case.

Adams's Hypothesis treats Simple Conditionals as *epistemic*, since a speaker's probability-function reflects his state of knowledge: an increase in knowledge typically carries with it a revision of his probability-assignments. Thus, Adams's theory can explain the fact already mentioned, that someone who knows only that at least one of P and Q is true, without knowing the truth of P and Q separately, may assert 'If not-P then Q', even if, for most people, P and Q are unconnected; whereas someone who knows that P is true may not be ready to assign any probability to Q's being the case in the event of P's falsehood.

It follows, by the probability calculus, that if the probability of Q given P is high, that of not-Q given P is low; so, 'If P then Q' and 'If P then not-Q' will not be jointly assertible by the same person. But it may be possible for 'If P then Q' and 'If P then not-Q' both to be assertible in the same context by different persons whose epistemic states, and therefore probability-functions, are different, as the following example, first introduced by Allan Gibbard, shows.[4] Sly Pete and Stone are playing poker on a Mississippi riverboat, and Pete is cheating, and has observed Stone's hand. An observer, Zack, may reasonably say, in advance of knowing who won, that if Pete called, he won, if he knows that Pete is cheating, and would call only if he had a winning hand; another onlooker, Jack, on the other hand, on the basis of a knowledge of Pete's and Stone's hands, may equally reasonably say, 'If Pete called, he lost,' knowing that Pete's hand was weaker than Stone's. This suggests that there is no asking whether 'If P

---

[4] Gibbard, 'Two Recent Theories of Conditionals', 211–47.

then Q' is assertible independently of a certain body of knowledge, whether that is that possessed by an individual speaker, or
a body presupposed as common to the participants in a discussion.

Similarly (as we saw in Section 1), I, knowing only that everyone at the meeting voted for the proposal, am entitled to say that
if Jones was present, he voted for the proposal. You, knowing
Jones's character and opinions, may, on the strength of *that* evidence, be equally entitled to say if Jones was present, he did *not*
vote for the proposal. Of course, if it turns out that Jones was
present, we cannot both be right: either my information was
incorrect or your evidence misled you. But if Jones was not present, it seems that we may each be correct in what we say, relative
as it was to different evidence.

We have seen that Prob(Q/P) is undefined when the probability of P is zero. This raises a problem for those cases in which P
is necessarily false, and known to be so by the speaker. We do
make use of Simple Conditionals with necessarily false
antecedents, particularly in mathematical contexts where we
argue by *reductio*, deriving contradictory consequences from a
necessarily false hypothesis. We may thus reasonably say something of the form,

'If the square root of 2 is rational, then . . .,'

where we apply a general truth to what is envisaged in the
antecedent of the conditional.

A difficulty may be raised about the Ramsey Test (and therefore about Adams's theory) from cases when someone is ready to
assert a conditional, but, on learning that the antecedent is true,
declines to infer that the consequent is true.[5] Thus, I may be ready
to say that if John is not at home, he is in his office, on the
strength of conditional probability, and continue to assert it even
though I have ascertained that John is not at the office. If I then
learn that John is not at home, I will decline to infer that he is in
his office (which I know is not the case), but instead cease to
accept the conditional. What this sort of case shows is that we
sometimes assert 'If P then Q', knowing Q to be false—

---

[5] See David Sanford, *If P, then Q: Conditionals and the Foundations of Reasoning* (London, 1989), 142–56.

knowledge that would not be undermined by the truth of the antecedent.

If Adams's Hypothesis predicts the assertibility-conditions of Simple Conditionals in a wide range of cases, several questions arise. Is an account of the assertibility-conditions of Simple Conditionals in terms of conditional probability the whole truth about their assertibility-conditions? And what explanation of the meaning of 'If . . . then . . .' will be given to harmonize with the phenomena which, in large measure, conform to Adams's Hypothesis? Do Simple Conditionals have truth-values, or should we accept the no-truth-value view of Adams and others? These are the topics of the next section.

# 4

# Simple Conditionals and
# Truth-Values: Some Proposals

Given that, as we saw in the last section, Prob(Q/P) is, in general, not equal to Prob(P ⊃ Q), and may in fact diverge from it considerably, we may be led by the apparent success of Adams's Hypothesis in explaining the phenomena to look for truth-conditions other than those of the material conditional; more specifically, we may look for truth-conditions for 'If P then Q' which ensure that the probability of its truth matches the relevant conditional probability. Indeed, it may seem that this is the only option, if Adams's suggestion is correct. It seems hard to accept that the probability of a proposition can be anything other than the probability of its truth. So, if the probability (and therefore, degree of assertibility) that we ascribe to 'If P then Q' is the probability of Q given P, 'If P then Q' should express a proposition the probability of whose truth matches that conditional probability.

Unfortunately, and perhaps rather surprisingly, David Lewis has shown that there is no such proposition: it is not possible to assign truth-conditions to 'If P then Q' that make the probability of its truth equal to the conditional probability of Q given P. Or rather, the identification of the probability of 'If P then Q' with the associated conditional probability will work only with trivial probability-functions, which do not assign positive probability to more than two pairwise incompatible propositions. If we assume that Prob(If P then Q) = Prob(Q/P), whatever probability-function is taken, it is possible, given standard assumptions of probability theory, to show that Prob(Q/P) = Prob(Q).[1] [For related results, see Dorothy Edgington's Commentary.]

---

[1] Cf. David Lewis, 'Probabilities of Conditionals and Conditional Probabilities', *Philosophical Papers*, ii. 133–58.

This result is sometimes said to be the result that there is no such proposition as the proposition that 'If P then Q' (compare Gibbard), because it shows that, assuming Adams's Hypothesis, and assuming also that probability is always probability of truth, there is no proposition the probability of whose truth always coincides with Prob(Q/P), whatever probability-function is taken. Lewis's triviality result narrows the options available.

One option, retaining the plausible view that the probability of a proposition must always be the probability of its truth, is to deny that Simple Conditionals express propositions. This leaves open the option of treating them as non-truth-valued conditional assertions, as Adams does.

Alternatively, we may hold that conditionals are an exception to the generalization that assertibility goes with probability of truth, and it is then open to us to assign truth-conditions to 'If P then Q'. That line is taken by Lewis, who holds that Simple Conditionals have the same truth-conditions as material conditionals.

It needs to be stressed, before we consider alternative suggestions, that Lewis's result does *not* show that, on each occasion when a speaker asserts that 'If P then Q', there is no proposition whose probability coincides with the conditional probability of Q given P. What Lewis showed is that there is no *single* proposition that 'If P then Q' expresses that will always have a probability that matches Prob(Q/P) no matter what probability-function is taken: it is ruled out that there should be a (non-extensional) sentence operator that fixes a content for 'If P then Q' as a function of the contents of P and Q, whose probability meets the required conditions. It is still left open that 'If P then Q' should express a proposition the probability of whose truth coincides with the relevant conditional probability, provided it is allowed that what proposition is expressed is not independent of a speaker's probability-function. 'If P then Q' will have truth-conditions, but they have to be assigned relative to the epistemic state of the person whose acceptance of 'If P then Q' is in question. This may make Lewis's result seem less paradoxical. Note that in the last section we saw some reason to allow that 'If P then Q' and 'If P then not-Q' may both be acceptable for speakers whose state of knowledge is relevantly different.

If, however, we allow that the truth-conditions of Simple

Conditionals do not *directly* fix their assertibility-conditions, can we treat them as equivalent to material conditionals? As we saw, one suggestion is to regard 'If P then Q' as equivalent in meaning to the material conditional, and offer a pragmatic explanation of their assertibility-conditions. So I begin by considering Grice's proposals.[2]

Grice appealed to a general principle governing conversational interchanges that one should not (normally) make the weaker of two assertions when one is in a position to make the stronger. The notion of what one is in a position to assert is explained in terms of evidence: a speaker is in a position to assert P when he has sufficient evidence for P, and, in accordance with established philosophical usage, P is said to be stronger than Q when P entails Q, but not vice versa. So the suggestion is that, if P entails Q, but not conversely, and one has sufficient evidence to be justified in asserting P (and therefore sufficient for Q also), it would be misleading, without special explanation, to assert Q rather than P, other things being equal.

This principle is held to apply to conversational exchanges because there is a presumption on the part of the participants in such an exchange that a speaker is trying to be as helpful as possible. (This is called a Co-operative Principle by Grice.) Though commonly made, the presumption may be defeated in certain circumstances. But, since it is made, a hearer is normally entitled to infer what would be the case if the speaker were observing the Co-operative Principle. Now (to put things briefly) he would not be being as helpful as he could be if he had almost equally good evidence for P and for Q, P and Q were each relevant to the purposes of the conversational exchange, but P was more helpful, because more informative. These conditions will be fulfilled when P entails Q, and the speaker has adequate evidence for P. Hence, if he is to adhere to the Co-operative Principle, the speaker must conform to the maxim mentioned earlier, of not making the weaker of two statements when he is in a position to make the stronger. Obviously, the maxim will not be conformed to without exception, and it is a merit of Grice's theory that it is not hard to see why that is so; there may be special factors.

[2] Grice, William James Lectures, in *Studies in the Way of Words*.

So, if a speaker makes the weaker of two statements, when the stronger of them would have been more helpful, a hearer is entitled to infer, on the assumption that the speaker is conforming to the Co-operative Principle, that he is not in a position to make the stronger because he lacks enough evidence; in short, he does not know whether it is true or false.

Now, if we interpret 'If P then Q' as a material conditional, it is entailed by 'Not-P' and by Q, but does not entail them. These statements are therefore stronger. Thus, the maxim would require that a speaker should not assert 'If P then Q' except in circumstances in which he does not know the truth-value either of P or of Q. But he would be in a position to assert 'If P then Q' despite ignorance of the truth-values of P and of Q only if there were some sort of connection between them. Hence, a hearer is entitled to infer that there is, or at least that the speaker believes that there is, some sort of connection between the truth-values of P and of Q. This is put by Grice by saying that the speaker *implicates* that there is such a connection. The existence of such a connection is a matter of *conversational implicature*: it is generated pragmatically, and is not attributable to the conventional meaning of 'If . . . then . . .'.

If the theory is to have plausibility, the claim that Co-operative Principles, attributable to conversational maxims, do in fact govern conversational exchanges, must not be simply *ad_hoc*. We should expect to find them operating elsewhere; and in fact, we can find another case in which the Gricean principles may plausibly be invoked which is of particular significance for the present case. It seems hard to dispute that the truth-conditions and meaning of a statement of the form 'Either P or Q' in natural language are precisely those given by the standard truth-table of the Propositional Calculus; yet it is easy to find cases in which it would be misleading for someone to assert something of the form 'Either P or Q' even though it would be true. If I am asked where Margaret is, and I know that she is in France, it would, standardly, be misleading for me to say that she is either in France or Italy. The latter remark would be appropriate, normally, only if I do not know which country she is in, though I know that she is in one or the other. The misleadingness would be particularly flagrant if, not only do I know (or think I know) that she is in

France, but I have no reason to think that, were it to turn out that she is not in France after all, she would prove to be in Italy.

There may, to be sure, be contextual reasons for someone to say 'Either P or Q' when he knows that one or other of those is true; perhaps he has a special reason for not being fully specific; if so, a hearer will not be misled if he knows this, or the speaker explicitly reports this. Thus, there is nothing in the meaning of 'Either . . . or . . .' which prevents someone from saying: 'Either P or Q, but I'm not telling you which.' This is surely a point in favour of a Gricean account of this feature of the use of disjunctive statements in English: the conversational implicature is *cancellable*. If one accepts, as almost everyone does, that the meaning of 'Either . . . or . . .' is purely truth-functional, any implication carried in any context that the speaker does not know the truth-value of either of the disjuncts must be generated pragmatically; and the most plausible account of the manner of generation is surely that in saying that you know that Margaret is in Italy or France when you know that she is in France, you are being less informative than you might have been. In being less informative, you are being less helpful to your interlocutor; and if your hearer assumes, instead, that you *are* being maximally informative, this must, presumably, be on general grounds.

We are thus led, starting with the almost uncontroversial thesis that the meaning of disjunctions is purely truth-functional, to adopt a Gricean explanation of certain phenomena. This shows that the Gricean explanation of Simple Conditionals is not *ad hoc*. Moreover, if one holds that the *meaning* of 'If . . . then . . .' is fully captured by the standard truth-table, any Simple Conditional will be fully equivalent to a disjunction, and therefore any implicatures generated pragmatically in the one case ought to be generated in the other, and it will be hardly possible to offer a different explanation of their generation: there will have to be the same explanation of the fact that one who asserts 'If P then Q' will standardly be taken not to know that P is false or that Q is true as there is of the fact that one who asserts 'Either P or Q' does not know the truth-values either of P or of Q.

However, the fact that we are normally not ready to assert 'Either P or Q' except when we would *not* be in a position either to assert P or to assert Q, reveals a weakness in the pragmatic explanation of the assertibility-conditions of 'If P then Q'. A disjunction is symmetrical, and any *general* constraint on asserting 'Either P or Q' when one is in a position to assert *one* of the disjuncts should apply equally to the other.[3]

Simple Conditionals exhibit an asymmetry, of which the grammatically subordinate character of the 'If'-clause is one manifestation. One way of seeing this is to note that there are reasons for regarding 'If P then Q' as an assertion of Q conditionally upon P, but not for seeing it as an assertion of not-P conditionally upon not-Q.

In the last section, it was suggested that there were powerful reasons for accepting Adams's Hypothesis that a Simple Conditional is assertible when the conditional probability of the consequent, given the antecedent, is high. There is no comparable argument for supposing that 'If P then Q' is assertible when the conditional probability of not-P, given not-Q, is high. Yet 'P ⊃ Q' is equivalent, if Grice's proposals are correct, in meaning to 'not-Q ⊃ not-P'; so any pragmatic, conversational implicature generated by one ought to be generated equally by the other.

Examples considered in the last section show that 'Either P or Q' may be assertible when 'If not-P then Q' is not; and likewise, 'If P then Q' may be assertible when 'If not-Q then not-P' is not. Several of the examples cited show that we are frequently ready to assert 'If P then Q' in circumstances in which we are also in a position to assert Q, a fact that will hardly be explained by the presumption that a speaker is being maximally informative.

Moreover, as Jackson points out, someone who accepts the truth of Q will not necessarily be ready to assert just *any* conditional of the form 'If P then Q', regardless of what P is; despite the fact that accepting Q commits him to accepting 'P ⊃ Q'. Even if I take myself to know that Peter was at the party, I shall not assert 'If I have been totally misinformed about it, Peter was at the party'. There seems to be no prospect of explaining on a Gricean basis the fact that we discriminate in our readiness to

---

[3] It is true that, in certain cases, someone *would* be prepared to assert one of the disjuncts, as we saw in the last section with 'He lives in Boston, or somewhere in New England', and perhaps 'It either rained or snowed in Berkeley last year'; but those examples are ones in which one disjunct would be true only if the other one was, and there is clearly no *general* asymmetry.

accept Simple Conditionals with consequents that we believe to be true.

We are thus led to postulate an element in the meaning of 'If . . . then . . .' that is not attributable to truth-conditions; so the question now arises how that feature of its meaning is to be characterized. Jackson, who accepts that Simple Conditionals are equivalent in truth-conditions to material conditionals, introduces a principle that is readily suggested by some of the examples discussed, of the *robustness* of a proposition relative to certain information. Intuitively, a proposition is robust with respect to certain information if the probability of its truth can withstand the discovery of that information. Thus, seeing a man in a monk's habit in the street, the probability that I shall assign to the hypothesis that he is a member of a religious order is going to be high. It will plummet, however, if I subsequently learn that a play is being put on locally in which a monk is one of the characters, and today is the day of the dress rehearsal. The probability that I assigned to his being a monk was not robust with respect to the new information.

Although all truths are compatible, and truth is not a matter of degree, and the truth of one thing is not in danger of being undermined by further truths, probability is notoriously rather different: the probability assignable to P may change in the light of new information. This reflects the fact that probability is relative to evidence. So, if we associate assertibility, as we have been doing, with a high degree of probability, what may be initially assertible may not be in the light of new information. Jackson defines *robustness* as follows: a proposition is robust with respect to information J if and only if the probability of P and of P given J are both high, and more or less the same.[4] Now a material conditional may or may not be robust with respect to the truth of the antecedent. If the probability of 'If P then Q', understood as a material conditional, is high, and further, its probability remains high relative to the truth of the antecedent, we can say that the conditional is robust with respect to the truth of the antecedent.

In such a case, $\text{Prob}((P \supset Q)/P)$ is hardly less than $\text{Prob}(P \supset Q)$. But it is an evident theorem of the probability calculus that $\text{Prob}((P \supset Q)/P) = \text{Prob}(Q/P)$. We have already seen that the

---

[4] Jackson, *Conditionals,* 22.

assertibility of a conditional is correlated with the associated conditional probability; we can now see that whether, when the probability of truth of a conditional is high, the corresponding conditional probability is high or not, depends on whether the conditional in question is robust with respect to the truth of its antecedent. So the explanations offered by Adams of the apparent failure of validity of inferences that are valid with the material conditional can be accommodated to the hypothesis that it is a semantic requirement for the assertibility of a Simple Conditional that it be robust with respect to its antecedent.

Two points may be noted about the merits of this notion of the robustness of a conditional with respect to its antecedent, in relation to Grice's theory.

First, the theory that robustness with respect to the antecedent is a condition for the assertibility of a Simple Conditional has all the success in explaining the divergence between their assertibility-conditions and their truth-conditions that Grice's theory had. Grice's principles seem to work for many cases where the probability of truth of the conditional is high, but that is mainly due to the probable falsehood of the antecedent. Such cases are typically those in which the probability of the conditional is high, but the associated conditional probability is low, or at any rate not high enough to make the conditional assertible, if assertibility is tied to conditional probability. These are cases in which the antecedent is false, and the consequent is something quite unconnected with it. In such cases, someone may know (have good evidence for, assign a high probability to) the falsehood of the antecedent, but if the consequent is unconnected, there will, in general, be no grounds for assigning a high probability to the truth of the conditional if the antecedent should prove to be true. Thus such conditionals are not robust with respect to the truth of their antecedents.

Secondly, however, we have already seen that some conditionals *are* assertible even though the probability of the material conditional is hardly greater than that of the falsehood of the antecedent (both being high), contrary to what would be predicted on the strength of the Gricean principle. These are cases in which the conditional probability is high—that is, the probability of the consequent, given the truth of the antecedent, is high, compared with the probability of the negation of the consequent, given the antecedent.

One reason for accepting that Simple Conditionals do have truth-conditions is that we are then in a position to give an explanation of complex sentences in which such conditionals occur within the scope of truth-functional connectives. Any theory that ascribes truth-values to conditionals can explain the meaning of sentences of the form 'If P, then, if Q then R' or 'If Q if P, then R', where conditionals are iterated, or 'Either if P then Q or if R then S', where conditionals occur within the scope of a truth-functional operator. If we are told that the whole truth about the use of 'If P then Q' is that it is used to make a conditional assertion, we are uninstructed on how to understand such sentences, for instance, those in which a conditional occurs as the antecedent of another conditional.

However, the view that Simple Conditionals have the same truth-conditions as material conditionals encounters problems when we consider complex conditionals such as those just mentioned: it is hard to see how the assertibility-conditions that we find them to have are generated.

In particular (and this was recognized by Grice to be a serious difficulty for his pragmatic explanation), the negation of a conditional will be equivalent to the conjunction of the antecedent with the negation of the consequent if the sole condition for the truth of 'If P then Q' is the truth of 'P ⊃ Q'; yet it seems that we *never* take one who denies 'If P then Q' to be committing himself to the truth of P and the falsehood of Q.

The question of embedded conditionals, and the question whether conditionals have a truth-value, will be taken up in Section 6. But first I will complete my survey of the available options by considering possible-worlds theories.

# 5

# Conditionals and Possible Worlds

In Section 2, I argued that one traditional piece of doctrine about conditionals is false: that there is a class of conditional statements—traditionally labelled 'counterfactual' or 'subjunctive'—which convey the implication, by the tense and mood of the verb, that the antecedent is false. But I also argued that there were good grounds for holding that there are two broad classes of conditionals to be distinguished, marked off from one another by a semantic difference.

What we need to do is to characterize the semantic differences marked by such features as the presence of 'would'. The question then arises how the two classes are to be distinguished. Given the falsehood of the Counterfactuality Thesis, it will not be satisfactory to use the implication of the antecedent's falsehood as a criterion.

Recently, the dominant approach to the analysis of 'counterfactual' conditionals has been one that makes use of possible worlds. The vogue that this approach enjoys is due particularly to the work of David Lewis and Robert Stalnaker.[1] Although I have rejected the Counterfactuality Thesis, I have recognized that 'counterfactual' conditionals are typically used by someone who believes the antecedent to be false. So an analysis in terms of possible worlds, in which provision is made for possible situations distinct from the actual, is naturally applied to them.

Lewis applies the possible-worlds apparatus only to 'counterfactual' conditionals, but Stalnaker (and others) apply the possible-worlds apparatus also to Simple Conditionals; the truth-conditions of 'counterfactual' conditionals are different—

---

[1] Lewis, *Counterfactuals*; Stalnaker, 'A Theory of Conditionals', in *Studies in Logical Theory*, American Philosophical Quarterly Monograph Series, No. 2 (Oxford, 1968), 98–112, reprinted in Harper, Stalnaker, and Pearce (eds.), *Ifs*, 41–55, and in Jackson (ed.), *Conditionals*, 28–45.

this being the significance of the difference in the forms of word used—but the possible-worlds apparatus is applied in both cases.[2]

Possible-worlds theories start from the natural thought that when a 'counterfactual' conditional is used, we envisage a possible state of affairs, typically distinct from the actual, in which the antecedent is true, and say that in *that* situation, the consequent is true also. Thus, in saying that if Hugh Gaitskell had survived in 1963, he would have been the Prime Minister instead of Harold Wilson, I imagine a possible state of affairs in which Gaitskell survives his illness in 1963, and claim that in the imagined state of affairs, he becomes Prime Minister.

It is clear that, to reach a definite conclusion about the truth of the consequent in the situation envisaged will require that the possible situation be sketched in sufficient detail for the consequent's truth-value to be fixed. Thus, in the example given, we shall have to envisage not only that Gaitskell survives but also that other aspects of the political scene are such as to lead to a Labour victory. We envisage a situation that includes Gaitskell's survival, but much else besides.

A natural next step is to introduce, instead of a possible *situation*—a way things might have been in certain respects—a possible *world*: a way the world might have been in every possible aspect, at any time. Such a possible world will typically coincide with the way things are in some respects, and diverge in others, and it will have all its details filled in: with respect to every way in which the world may be, such a world is determinately thus or not thus. It is evident that one way the world may be is the way that it actually is. So one among the countless possible worlds is the actual world.

In conformity with this, propositions will be true or false in a given possible world, as the case may be. In the possible world described above 'Gaitskell died in 1963' will be false, as will all the other propositions that entail it; others will be true that are false in the actual world. A proposition's being true or false *simpliciter* will consist in its being true or false in one particular possible world—the actual world.

---

[2] [Woods resumes the discussion of Simple Conditionals half-way through this section and at the beginning of the next.]

The suggestion is that when accepting a 'counterfactual' conditional, we envisage a world in which its antecedent is true. But plainly there is no single world in which the antecedent is true, but countless worlds which agree in this feature but differ in others. Moreover, except when the consequent is entailed by, or is inconsistent with, the antecedent, among worlds in which the antecedent is true, there will be some in which the consequent is true and others in which it is false. Thus, there will be some worlds in which Abraham Lincoln is not assassinated by Booth, but he is assassinated by someone else, and history takes a course not greatly unlike its actual course; in others, he is not assassinated at all, and the course of history diverges more sharply from the actual. So, if the question whether the consequent is true in the possible world envisaged is to have a determinate answer, some selection must be made from those worlds that include the antecedent's truth.

A first suggestion might be that the context determines which possible world is chosen.[3] Reflection upon some examples may support this suggestion: in the case of some conditionals, there seems to be no determinate way of settling the question of their truth-value if they are considered outside a context which makes more determinate what counterfactual supposition is being entertained. Is it true or false that if John were out of the country now he would be in France? There may be various alternative scenarios in which John leaves the country, some of which take him to France and some of which do not. Only contextual determination will yield a definite answer. Similarly with a pair of examples first introduced by Quine:

> If Bizet and Verdi were compatriots, Bizet and Verdi would both be French,

and

> If Bizet and Verdi were compatriots, Bizet and Verdi would both be Italian.

Unless it is made determinate *how* the two composers are envis-

---

[3] It would be more realistic to speak, instead, of a *set* of possible worlds, since there will always be a large number of worlds that are alike in all respects relevant to the truth of the conditional.

aged as being compatriots, there is no choosing between these
rival conditionals.[4]

What these examples suggest is that there are 'counterfactual'
conditionals on whose truth-value we cannot decide, and not
because of any lack of knowledge on our part. In so far as we *do*
arrive at a decision, this must be because the context indicates
*which* possible world in which the antecedent is true the speaker
is considering. However, as Lewis has argued, in a large number
of cases no contextual determination is required to yield a determinate answer. We may be ready to regard

'If John had worked harder he would have got a First'

as definitely true, without any contextual assumptions, even
though there are possible worlds in which John works harder but
fails to get a First; for example, because John's ability is different,
or the performance required for a First is higher than it is in the
actual world.

It seems, then, that we have a general, not context-relative,
procedure for choosing among worlds in which the antecedent of
the conditional is true. We consider worlds in which, as far as
possible, everything is as it is in the actual world apart from the
truth-value of the antecedent. As Lewis says:

'If kangaroos had no tails, they would topple over' seems to me to mean
something like this: in any possible state of affairs in which kangaroos
have no tails, and which resembles our actual state of affairs as much as
kangaroos having no tails permits it to, the kangaroos topple over.[5]

It is evidently impossible to have *everything* exactly as it is in
the actual world apart from the truth of the antecedent. Thus,
any world in which (contrary to fact) I arrive at my appointment
on time instead of two hours late will have to be one that differs
from the actual world in *other* ways; either I left earlier or the
time of the appointment was later or technology was more
advanced so as to allow a drastically faster journey or the laws of
physics were different or . . .. So it is natural to hold that we
always consider a world which is as like the actual as is allowed
by the difference in truth-value of the antecedent.

[4] See W. V. O. Quine, *Methods of Logic*, 3rd edn. (London, 1974), 21.
[5] See *Counterfactuals*, 1.

This way of putting the matter carries with it the idea that possible worlds other than the actual can be *ordered* with respect to their closeness or similarity to the actual: we consider the world that is as like the actual as possible, which presupposes that it should make sense to ask which of two worlds is more like the actual. So, as appears from the passage from Lewis recently quoted, the suggestion is that 'If P had been the case, Q would have been the case' (or some variant of that) is true if and only if Q is true in the closest world to the actual in which P is true, where *closeness* is understood as *similarity* to the actual.

A theory along these lines will explain why we have a breakdown of inferences that are valid with the material conditional similar to that which we had with Simple Conditionals: the reason is that there is no reason why the world closest to the actual in which *one* antecedent is true is the same as that in which other antecedents are. Thus we reject

> 'If he had not been wearing a seatbelt, he would have been killed in the accident. If he had gone to work by bus, he would not have been wearing a seatbelt. Therefore, if he had gone to work by bus, he would have been killed.'

The closest possible world in which he does not wear a seatbelt is one in which he travels in his own car, as in the actual world; a world in which he travels by bus is less close to the actual, and in that the consequent of the first premiss may not be true. Similarly, Q may be true in the closest world in which P is true, but false in the closest world (less close to the actual) in which 'P and R' is. So, 'If P had been the case, Q would have been the case' may be true when 'If P and R had been the case, Q would have been the case' is false.

This proposal raises a number of questions: First, can we reasonably assume that there is a single world *closest* to the actual in which the antecedent is true? We might think that there are sometimes several such worlds each of which is as close to the actual as any world is; and if so, the consequent might be true in some of them and false in others. Lewis calls the assumption that there is always a single such closest world the Uniqueness Assumption. But need there always be a world or set of worlds in which the antecedent is true, each as close as any is to the actual? Perhaps, given any such world in which the antecedent is true, it is always possible to find one that is closer still to the actual. If we hold that that is not so, we are making what Lewis calls the Limit Assumption.

Second, what if the antecedent of a 'counterfactual' conditional is *true*? As we saw in Section I, though Lewis holds that these conditionals are appropriately used only if the antecedent is false, he does not regard it as part of what is strictly said by such an utterance that the antecedent is false; so 'counterfactual' conditionals are not to be treated as all false when they have true antecedents. In fact, if we apply truth-conditions of the kind proposed by Lewis and Stalnaker to 'counterfactual' conditionals with a true antecedent, it seems that such conditionals will come out as true or false according to whether the consequent is true or false; for it seems reasonable to hold that the world closest to the actual world is the actual world itself, and hence the closest world in which the antecedent is true, if the antecedent is in fact true, is the actual world itself. The assumption that the world closest to the actual world absolutely is the actual world itself, is called by Lewis the Centring Assumption.

Third, what if the antecedent is necessarily false, i.e. there are no possible worlds in which it is true? Lewis holds that all such conditionals are vacuously true; and indeed the truth-conditions proposed may reasonably be taken to admit of vacuous fulfilment: trivially, any world closest to the actual in which P is true is one in which Q is true, for any Q, if there are no worlds in which P is true.

Problems are raised by all three of these issues. It is hardly plausible to hold that our ways of assessing worlds for closeness to the actual world suffice to justify either the Limit or the Uniqueness Assumption. I may suppose, contrary to fact, that I encountered some acquaintance on a journey, which might have come about in countless ways that would have preserved close similarity to the actual world; but it is hardly plausible to hold that we recognize just *one* of the scenarios that would have made the antecedent true as closer to the actual than any other. Accordingly, rather than saying that a 'counterfactual' conditional is true if the world closest to the actual in which the antecedent is true is one in which the consequent is true also, it may be preferable to say instead, as Lewis does, that it is true if the consequent is true in some antecedent-verifying world that is closer than any in which the consequent is false; this carries no commitment to the Limit or Uniqueness Assumptions. But then, if in some closest worlds in which P is true, Q is also true, and in some Q is false, 'If P had been the case, Q would have been the case' will be false, and so will 'If P had been the case, Q would not have been the case'. Thus, Lewis is committed to a denial of what has sometimes been called Conditional Excluded Middle: the thesis that, for all P and Q, either, if P had been the case, Q would have been the case, or, if P had been the case, Q would not have been the case. Our intuitions may be thought to favour acceptance of such a law: it may seem strange to say that 'If Hannibal had marched on Rome, he would have taken it' and 'If Hannibal had marched on Rome, he would not have taken it' could both be false.

If we make the Uniqueness Assumption, then it is a matter of course that if the consequent is true in the single closest antecedent-permitting world, the consequent's negation must be false. So Conditional Excluded Middle will hold. As an alternative to the simple Uniqueness Assumption, we may think that, even though that Assumption is hardly defensible in general, it is *presupposed* by someone who uses a 'counterfactual' conditional that there is some one possible world closest to the actual in which the antecedent in question is true. When I say that if Jones had been present, he would have voted for the proposal, I am saying that in the situation that most resembles the way things actually are in which Jones is present, *assuming that there is one*, he voted in favour. If that assumption does not hold, the conditional in question (and likewise its contrary) is neither true nor false. This suggestion surely has considerable plausibility.

The main argument against counting all 'counterfactual' conditionals with true antecedents as true if their consequents are true is similar to the standard arguments against treating Simple Conditionals as material conditionals: it would require us to hold as true 'counterfactual' conditionals with unrelated antecedent and consequent that we should not normally use.[6]

---

[6] As already indicated, it seems that our intuitions about the truth and falsehood of some bizarre examples are not very clear. Moreover, it is in fact possible to avoid that consequence by revising and weakening what Lewis calls the Centring Assumption, and saying not that the actual world is closer to itself than any other world is, but only that no world is closer to it than it is to itself.

Rather more serious problems are raised by Lewis's treatment of 'counterfactual' conditionals with impossible antecedents. It appears that we do use such conditionals, knowing the antecedent to be impossible. One example, mentioned already, is in mathematical reasoning: 'If the square root of two had been rational . . .', where a certain hypothesis is reduced to absurdity. Again, someone may initiate a speculation with 'If I had been born in the eighteenth century . . .'; yet, if one accepts the claim that what a thing comes from it necessarily comes from, maybe there is no possible world in which I am born in the eighteenth century. We do use such conditionals, however, and we adopt a discriminating attitude towards their truth-values: not every such conditional with an impossible antecedent is thought to be true, as is evident from the mathematical examples.

Like Lewis, Stalnaker confronts the problem of selecting *which* possible world in which the antecedent is true is relevant to the assessment of such conditionals; but instead of basing that choice on the relation of similarity to the actual world, he introduces the notion of a Selection Function. Relative to any possible world taken as being actual, there is a function that maps each proposition that may occur as the antecedent of a 'counterfactual' conditional on to exactly one world, and the conditional is true if and only if the consequent is true in the world picked out by the relevant Selection Function.

Will the relation of similarity do the work required of it in Lewis's theory? General questions may be raised about the very idea of comparing worlds in respect of similarity, given that the possible respects of similarity between worlds are so diverse, and it depends so much on our interests and purposes which points of resemblance are regarded as crucial. None the less, it surely seems hard to deny that we are in a position sometimes to judge that a world A is closer to B than C is. Problems do arise, however, with conditionals whose antecedents concern particular events with diverse and far-reaching consequences. Consider a conditional beginning 'If Booth had not shot Abraham Lincoln . . .'. One natural thought is that the course of American history would have been very different in countless ways if it had been true. But is the closest (most similar) world in which Booth does not shoot Lincoln one which diverges from the actual in all the ways in which we think that things would have been different if the counterfactual antecedent had been fulfilled? It is surely possible to envisage a possible world in which Booth does not shoot Lincoln, but in most other respects history is as it is in the actual world. We could envisage Lincoln dying of a heart attack, or someone else shooting him on the very same occasion as Booth did. Likewise, I may readily say, 'If I had accepted that job, I should now be in Australia'; but surely the *closest* world to the actual world is one in which I accept the job, but, for some reason, fail to take it up, and I remain where I am, and everything continues almost exactly as it does now. Quite generally, when we confidently make a judgement of the form 'If X had been the case, matters thereafter would have been very different' it seems that we can readily envisage a possible world in which, though X happens, other compensating divergences from the actual ensure that things continue very much as before.

These examples suggest that our natural judgements of comparative similarity of alternative worlds to the actual do not yield, using the truth-conditions proposed, the truth-value ascriptions to 'counterfactual' conditionals that we require. Lewis's response to this is to say that in applying his proposed truth-conditions, we should not be guided by our intuitive, pre-theoretical judgements of similarity between worlds; rather, our truth-value assignments to such conditionals are to be used to define the relation of similarity that he claims we operate with in assessing 'counterfactual' conditionals. Reflection on examples like the case of Abraham Lincoln suggest that we *order* the respects in which an alternative possible world may resemble the actual: certain points of similarity count more heavily than others. As we saw, it is possible for the total course of history to be much the same as it actually was in a world in which Booth did not assassinate Lincoln. But coincidence with the actual world *after* the time when, in fact, Lincoln was shot can be secured only if certain adjustments are made earlier: we have to introduce an alternative assassin, or make the circumstances different from the actual in the respect required to produce the same later history as in the actual world *after* the time of the occurrence described in the antecedent. So although we seem to be able to describe a possible world which matches the actual in most significant respects *apart from* Booth's failure to shoot, in that world there is not the coincidence with the actual at all times almost up to the moment of Booth's pulling the trigger that there is in the possible world that seems to be the relevant one for the conditional in question: namely, one in which *everything* coincides with the actual world until shortly before the trigger was pulled, and then, because of that coincidence, there is a major divergence later. Given that everything was just the same up to the final moment just before Booth pulled the trigger, a failure on Booth's part to shoot would be enough to yield a considerable difference in later history: it would be enough, that is, assuming the same laws of nature as there are in the actual world.

Accordingly, Lewis suggests that our intuitive judgements about the truth-values of these conditionals are respected if we give more weight to exact similarity over a limited period than to approximate similarity throughout, and more weight to coincidence in laws than to coincidence in particular facts.[7] The possible world in which Booth does not shoot Lincoln which has the same laws as the actual, and in which the coincidence with the actual is the greatest, is precisely the world which, as we saw, seems to be the world we consider when evaluating the conditional: one in which everything occurs as it actually does until the time of the antecedent, and then events unfold, in accordance with laws, in a way that deviates dramatically from the actual. Given the priority among aspects of similarity described, such a world is the one that most resembles the actual.

The idea of a possible world that meets these requirements of similarity to the actual presents difficulties. Can there be a world in which the natural laws are the same as they are in the actual world, which coincides with the actual for a substantial period up to a time shortly before the time of the antecedent, and in which the antecedent is true? It only requires a limited degree of local determinism for this suggestion to founder in incoherence. If everything is the same as in the actual world up to a time shortly before that of the antecedent, it will not be consistent with natural laws that the antecedent should be true. This is most clearly illustrated in cases in which it falls outside human agency whether the antecedent is fulfilled. Take:

---

[7] Cf. 'Counterfactual Dependence and Time's Arrow', *Noûs*, 13 (1979), 455–76; reprinted in Lewis, *Philosophical Papers*, ii. 32–52.

> 'If it had rained yesterday afternoon, the match would have been cancelled.'

In a possible world that matches the actual up to midday yesterday, rain is already excluded by laws of nature.

Lewis confronts this difficulty, and says that what we really envisage in such cases is a possible world that agrees with the actual in its laws, and coincides with the actual world in other respects up to a moment shortly before the relevant time, and then a 'small miracle' occurs,[8] so that the antecedent is true. Thus, to choose an example that *does* involve human agency, given things obtaining just before Lincoln was shot, with Booth's intentions as they were, only by a miracle could it have come about that Booth did not pull the trigger.

It certainly must be conceded that, at least in those sequences of occurrences that we take to be law-governed, we cannot coherently have the antecedent's fulfilment preceded by a sequence of events that matches those of the actual world, but without any breach of the laws of nature.

It is noticeable that the miracle postulated in the examples given is a small one; the antecedent's fulfilment would require only a small deviation from natural law. Lewis appeals to this in order to give an explanation of certain temporal asymmetries that appear in the way that we use 'counterfactual' conditional. Attention was first drawn to these by P. B. Downing.[9] To adapt Downing's example, consider

> 'If James had quarrelled with Mary yesterday, she would not have asked him for help today.'

Such a conditional presents no difficulties for the possible-worlds treatment: the closest possible world in which they quarrel yesterday is, we may suppose, one in which she does not ask his help today. But now consider

> 'If Mary had asked James for help today, they would not have quarrelled yesterday.'

---

[8] ['Small miracle' relative to the laws of the *actual* world, that is. Lewis does not believe in the possibility of occurrences in a world *w* which violate the laws of nature of *w*.]

[9] P. B. Downing, 'Subjunctive Conditionals, Time Order, and Causation', *Proceedings of the Aristotelian Society*, 59 (1958–9), 125–40.

Such a conditional strikes us bizarre; we do not normally use such a backward 'counterfactual' conditional. Other examples that display a similar bizarreness are:

> 'If the match had been cancelled, it would have rained yesterday afternoon.'

> 'If John had got a First, he would have worked hard.'

> 'If Jones had voted for the proposal, he would have been present at the meeting.'

The bizarreness seems to be attributable to the fact that the relation of dependence (and therefore also the temporal order) between the states of affairs specified in the antecedent and consequent is reversed.

It is worth noting that there is no such asymmetry with Simple Conditionals:

> 'If Jones voted for the proposal, he was present at the meeting'

is no more *outré* than

> 'If Jones was present at the meeting, he voted for the proposal.'

Now, taking the last example, the possible-worlds theory seems to have problems in explaining why we are reluctant to admit the back-tracking conditional, since, according to the judgement of similarity we are most inclined to make, the closest possible world in which Jones voted for the proposal is one in which he attends the meeting.

Lewis suggests that we regard a world in which a single small miracle occurs as closer to the actual world than one with a large miracle, or a large number of small ones. In general, at least in worlds like ours, a small deviation may allow the antecedent to be true despite coincidence for most of the time up to then; but if it has been fulfilled, its consequences ramify outwards, and any world in which the antecedent is true must differ from the actual in a large number of ways, that multiply with the passage of time. This means that, if the antecedent had been fulfilled at a particular time, coincidence thereafter with the actual world could be secured only at the cost of a multitude of occurrences that are miraculous from the point of view of the laws of the actual world. For this reason we regard the closest world as that one which matches the actual world up to the time of the antecedent, but diverges subsequently.

If that is correct, we can explain, Lewis holds, a certain asymmetry of counterfactual dependence: the fact that events after a given time depend on what occurs at that time in a way that what happens before it does not. When we envisage the world as different in some specific way from the way that it actually was, we think of earlier events as they actually are, with later events deviating in accordance with the laws we recognize, and this is so despite the fact that there is a symmetrical law-governed determination by events at one time of events at other times.

This will then explain the phenomenon already mentioned: we do not have much use for backtracking conditionals like

> 'If Jones had won a lot of money in that race, he would have bet upon Beginner's Luck.'

The explanation will be that we envisage the fulfilment of the antecedent after a preceding history that coincides with the actual; hence we are not ready to consider how different things would have been *earlier* if a certain counterfactual supposition had been fulfilled.[10]

As explained at the beginning, although the possible worlds

---

[10] Lewis does not deny that such back-tracking conditionals occur; but he holds that they require a special resolution of the question which alternative possible world in which the antecedent is true is to be considered, since the normal resolution would preserve past coincidence with the actual world. But he recognizes that such back-tracking involves special forms of words. Rather than saying

> 'If he had arrived on time, he would have caught the train,'

we say,

> 'If he had arrived on time, that could only have been because he caught the train,'

or,

> 'If he had arrived on time, he would have had to have caught the train.'

But the effect of such forms of words is to make the conditional not a back-tracking conditional after all. Such sentences do not say that if something had been the case at one time, something else would have been the case *earlier*; they say that if something had been the case, it would (then) have had a certain explanation, or that (then) something would have needed to have happened earlier.

apparatus is held by some philosophers to explain only 'counter-factual' conditionals, others have applied it to Simple Condition-als also. With such an application, we have a theory that assigns truth-conditions to Simple Conditionals without making them material conditionals. Stalnaker holds that in Simple, no less than in 'counterfactual', conditionals we consider possible worlds in which the antecedent is true; the difference lies in the fact that with 'counterfactual' conditionals, we consider possible worlds that deviate more sharply from the actual. When we assert a Simple Conditional, we consider only those possible worlds in which those things are assumed to be the case that are taken for granted, or presupposed, in the context (as, in the Kennedy example, it was presupposed that *someone* killed Kennedy);[11] whereas the 'counterfactual' form of words serves as a signal that that constraint is not being observed (as indeed it *cannot* be if the antecedent is known to be false) and that is the explanation for the asymmetry of acceptability between

> 'If Oswald had not killed Kennedy, someone else would have done'

and

> 'If Oswald did not kill Kennedy, someone else did.'

An alternative view, proposed by Wayne Davis, is that, in the case of Simple Conditionals, we simply consider that possible world which is most similar over all times to the actual, whereas with 'counterfactual' conditionals, we consider that which coin-cides with the actual up to the time of the antecedent.[12]

Against Stalnaker, it may be argued that we do not observe the proposed constraint on Simple Conditionals, and for the same reason as conformity to such a constraint is not possible in the case of typical 'counterfactual' conditionals. (Many Simple Conditionals are assertible whose antecedent is believed false.) Even in a context in which it is a presupposition accepted by

---

[11] See Robert Stalnaker, 'Indicative Conditionals', *Philosophia*, 5 (1975), 269–86; reprinted in Harper, Stalnaker, and Pearce (eds.), *Ifs*, 193–210, and in Frank Jackson (ed.), *Conditionals*, 136–54.

[12] Wayne A. Davis, 'Indicative and Subjunctive Conditionals', *Philosophical Review*, 88 (1979), 544–64.

speaker and hearer that I have not been misinformed, I can hardly decline to accept

> 'If Mary has left-wing views, I have been totally misinformed.'[13]

Quite generally, we see nothing unacceptable about a conditional of the form, 'If P is the case, certain things are not so that we have been taking for granted.'[14]

In a similar way, Davis's suggestion confronts the same problem that led to Lewis's ordering of possible worlds in respect of similarity. Believing that the witnesses are trustworthy, I may accept

> 'If the accused is innocent, many of the witnesses are lying.'

But the world that is most similar to the actual world, as I believe it to be, in which the accused is innocent, may be one in which the witnesses were trustworthy, but gave different testimony.

More generally, as we saw in Section 2, 'If P then Q' is normally assertible by someone who has grounds for the material conditional that are not sufficient either for not-P or for Q; but, in many such cases, the P-verifying possible world that is most like the actual will be one in which Q has whatever truth-value it actually has, irrespective of whether or not P is the case. Taking the earlier example, I may be ready to assert

> 'If the janitor was speaking the truth, no one left the building all night.'

But, if the consequent is in fact false, the closest possible world with janitorial veracity may well be one in which the consequent is still false, but the janitor said something different.

The importation of possible worlds into the analysis of Simple and 'counterfactual' conditionals alike fails to do justice to the epistemic character of Simple Conditionals which is reflected in the Ramsey Test, or to the apparently non-epistemic character of 'counterfactuals', which was noted in Section 2. In deciding whether to accept a Simple Conditional, I imagine a revision of

---

[13] Note that in such a case I should *not* say, ' If Mary had had left-wing views, I would have been totally misinformed.'

[14] See Jackson, 'Conditionals and Possibilia'.

my beliefs that involves the adding to them of a belief in the antecedent's truth; whereas, in evaluating a 'counterfactual', I carry out an imaginative revision of how things are.

Dissatisfaction may also be felt with a possible-worlds treatment of 'counterfactual' conditionals. We saw that there was a problem for Lewis in admitting a possible world in which past history is the same as in the actual world up to the time of the antecedent, and the laws are the same, without postulating a minor miracle. But it seems natural to hold that, in supposing the antecedent to be fulfilled, we need not have any belief about how that might have come about. We simply imagine its fulfilment, with background circumstances and past history otherwise much the same as they actually are, or so it seems. Bennett suggests that we make it part of the analysis of 'counterfactual' conditionals that the laws of the actual world are retained, along with the truth of the antecedent.[15] What we consider is that causally possible world which is closest to the actual world at the time relevant to the antecedent. Closeness is taken to imply similarity, but is not defined in terms of it. We can say that 'If P had been the case, Q would have been the case' asserts that Q is the case at all the causally possible worlds that are closest to the actual at the time of the antecedent.[16]

Bennett's theory dispenses with the need to envisage a miracle, in order for the antecedent to be fulfilled; we simply need to choose those worlds that are closest to the actual world at the time of the antecedent's envisaged fulfilment. But it imports the notion of a law into the analysis of these conditionals, whereas, for Lewis, laws are relevant to the evaluation of the truth-value of 'counterfactual' conditionals only because they are relevant to assessments of similarity.

Is the reference to possible worlds still essential? As Bennett recognizes, it depends whether the relation of similarity is taken as fundamental. If the relation of closeness between possible worlds is not explained in terms of similarity, the theory can be reformulated as a metalinguistic theory in the style of Nelson

---

[15] Cf. Jonathan Bennett, 'Counterfactuals and Temporal Direction', *Philosophical Review*, 93 (1984), 57–91.

[16] To say that a world is causally possible is, of course, to say that it is a world like the actual world in its laws.

Goodman.[17] Instead of speaking of closest causally possible worlds in which P is true, we can speak instead of what is derivable from P, in virtue of the laws of nature, together with certain other true premisses satisfying certain conditions, these conditions being the conditions for co-tenability with P (in Goodman's terminology). Only certain truths are admissible in deriving Q from P in accordance with causal laws, namely those which, intuitively speaking, would still hold if P were true; and the problem of defining co-tenability is the counterpart, in this theory, of the problem of defining what is the case in the closest worlds in which the antecedent is true, or of defining which are the closest worlds. We can then regard the idiom of possible worlds, of differing closeness to the actual, as dispensable in favour of one that speaks instead of what is derivable from the hypothesis of the antecedent's truth, together with other truths causally compatible with it. On the other hand, if closeness in glossed in terms of similarity, possible worlds are indispensable as items between which the relation holds.

Although Bennett's theory can avoid the appeal to possible worlds if closeness is not explained in terms of similarity, it seems to be open to some objection. First, the inclusion of an explicit reference to laws in the analysis means that it cannot apply to some 'counterfactual' conditionals concerning how things would have been if the laws of nature had been different. A theory that uses similarity between possible worlds can consider worlds like the actual except for some of the laws of nature ('If the force of gravity were halved . . .').

Secondly, Bennett's theory does not make provision for the temporal asymmetry mentioned earlier, which Bennett rejects. On the theory he proposes, a 'counterfactual' conditional is evaluated as true if the causally possible worlds in which the antecedent is true are ones in which the consequent is also true, and the consequent may concern either earlier or later times. So the theory contains no explanation of why conditionals like

> 'If these plants had flourished, they would have been planted in different soil'

are unacceptable.

---

[17] See *Fact, Fiction, and Forecast*, ch. I.

Thirdly, Bennett's theory, like Lewis's, provides no explanation of why some 'counterfactual' conditionals with impossible antecedents are regarded as acceptable and some not.

Should we, then, accept a theory like Lewis's? Even if a relation of comparative similarity between possible worlds can be defined that yields plausible truth-value assignments for these conditionals, the question still arises *why* we have this notion of similarity. More generally, why do we engage in the practice of considering possible worlds alternative to the actual in the way that we do? We need, first, to consider the reasons we have for examining, retrospectively, contrary-to-fact possibilities: what is the *point* of asking ourselves how things would have been if certain matters had been different? Further, we need to attend more closely to the specific features of 'counterfactual' conditionals: what is their logical form?

As a preliminary to this, I will develop an account of 'If . . . then . . .', on the basis of the discussion in earlier sections, with a view to explaining the purport of 'counterfactual' conditionals by it together with the specific characteristics of the 'counterfactual' form of words.

# 6

# Compound Conditionals and
# Truth-Values

If the conclusions of the last section are correct, that it is misguided to import possible worlds into the analysis of Simple Conditionals, what account should be given of them? What possibilities remain?

As we saw in Section 4, we may hold that Simple Conditionals lack truth-values, and that the correct account of them is that they are used to make conditional assertions: one who utters 'If P then Q' makes no unconditional assertion using this form of words, but asserts Q on condition that P. If we use Frege's assertion sign ' ⊢ ', an assertion of P will be represented by ' ⊢P', and an appropriate notation for the conditional assertion theory would be to represent 'If P then Q' by ⊢$_P$Q. As we saw in Section 4, the combined effect of Lewis's result and the acceptance of Adams's Hypothesis may suggest this as an appropriate treatment of Simple Conditionals. The conditions for an utterance of Q would be that the probability of Q is high relative to the truth of P.

Alternatively, it may be thought better to follow Lewis in accepting a divergence between the assertibility of conditionals and the probabilities of their truth, and assign the Simple Conditionals the truth-conditions of the material conditional, but regard them as subject to further conditions of assertibility, attributable to the semantic properties of 'If . . . then . . .', as described in Section 4. One such account is Jackson's, in terms of robustness; but it is also possible to offer a different explanation of the contribution of the semantic properties of 'If . . . then . . .' to their assertibility-conditions, an explanation of which has as a consequence that they are assertible only when they have the property of robustness.

We could hold, for example, that one who asserts 'If P then Q' asserts the material conditional (such being the truth-conditions of 'If P then Q'), but that, in virtue of the semantic properties of 'If . . . then . . .', such an utterance is a conditional assertion of Q on condition that P. This seems to impose the same assertibility-conditions as Jackson's explanation in terms of robustness.

Yet another alternative, as we saw in Section 4, is to assign truth-conditions that are not those of the material conditional, and circumvent Lewis's result by relativizing what is said to the epistemic state of the speaker.

In this section, I consider conditionals occurring as constituents of longer sentences—including conditionals embedded in other conditionals. Such conditionals present problems both for those who do, and for those who do not, assign conditionals truth-conditions.

The problem for those who do not assign truth-conditions is that, if you simply assign them assertibility-conditions, you don't settle how such conditionals are to be understood when they occur, for example, as the antecedent of another conditional, or in a 'that'-clause after a verb of propositional attitude. Such theorists are in the habit of saying that there is no need to assign truth-conditions to 'If P then Q', because if one simply gives an account of when 'If P then Q' may be asserted, that is all that anyone needs to know about the way in which Simple Conditionals are used. The trouble is that, if someone simply knows when 'If P then Q' may be asserted, they are quite uninstructed on how to understand 'It's not the case that if P then Q'. Stating assertibility-conditions gives us no information on how to understand them as inputs to longer sentences. If one simply holds that 'If P then Q' is fully explained by saying that it is used to assert Q conditionally upon P, there is no explanation of its occurrences when it is not used to make any sort of assertion, conditional or not.

Lewis puts it like this:

I have no conclusive objection to the hypothesis that indicative conditionals are non-truth-valued sentences, governed by a special rule of assertibility that does not involve their non-existent probabilities of truth. I have an inconclusive objection, however: the hypothesis requires too much of a fresh start, it burdens us with too much work still to be done, and wastes too much that has been done already. So far, we have nothing but a rule of assertibility for conditionals with truth-valued antecedents and consequents. But what about compound sentences that have such conditionals as constituents? We think we know how the truth-conditions for compound sentences of various kinds are determined by the truth-conditions of constituent sentences, but this knowledge would be useless if any of those subsentences lacked truth-conditions. Either we need new semantic rules for many familiar connectives and operators when applied to indicative conditionals—perhaps rules of truth, perhaps special rules of assertibility like the rule for conditionals themselves—or else we need to explain away all seeming examples of compound sentences with conditional constituents.[1]

On the other hand, a view like Jackson's has problems too. Given that they are assigned truth-values, there ought to be no difficulty in understanding their contribution to the content of sentences involving truth-functional sentence composition; nor generally to forms of compounding in which the content of the whole sentence reflects the content of the embedded sentences as fixed by their truth-conditions. But, if we reject Grice's view, and hold that Simple Conditionals are not equivalent in meaning to material conditionals, we are led to ask, when such a conditional occurs as a part of a longer sentence, how the extra element in the meaning of 'If' contributes to its meaning.

Further, if we consider actual examples of embedded conditionals, it appears that the truth-value of the sentences containing them is not determined in the way it would be if their truth-conditions were those of the material conditional. Some have suggested that in fact we have little use for embedded conditionals—certainly not for conditionals as antecedents to further conditionals. Dummett has argued that we tie the ascription of truth and falsehood to a form of words closely to whether or not sentences of that form can occur as the antecedents of conditionals:[2] he says that we have little use for conditionals as the antecedents of conditionals, and hence the ascription of truth or falsehood to them is problematic. In fact, it seems that we can find plenty of examples of conditionals as antecedents to other conditionals.

Take the following examples:

---

[1] 'Probabilities of Conditionals and Conditional Probabilities', *Philosophical Papers*, ii. 141–2.
[2] In *Frege: Philosophy of Language* (London, 1973), 349.

'If John accepted the job if he was offered it, there is nothing about his behaviour that anyone would think surprising.'

'If the building was made of stone if it was built before 1700, it clearly isn't the building that we saw.'

'If he drank orange juice if he drank anything, he didn't get drunk.'

However, Dummett's other claim, that there is a close connection between the question whether a form of words expresses something to which a truth-value may be assigned and whether it can occur as the antecedent of a conditional, has considerable plausibility, and we shall return to it later.

One problem, then, on a view like Jackson's, lies in explaining how to take account of the additional element of the meaning of 'If' that is not captured by its truth-conditions, when a conditional occurs embedded in a longer sentence.[3] Jackson's claim was that, in asserting 'If P then Q', I signal that the truth of what I say (understood as equivalent to a material conditional) is robust with respect to the truth of the antecedent. This, of course, *is* a rule of assertibility: it lays down conditions for the assertion 'If P then Q'. So how does this carry over to embedded conditionals?

---

[3] The paradigm of a construction whose meaning is not fully explained by giving the truth-conditions is, of course, 'P but Q', which differs in meaning from 'P and Q' though the truth-conditions are the same. Take

'If she was born in Turin, but left when she was three, she doesn't know Italy well.'

'Either he arrived on time but gave up waiting for us, or he never arrived at all.'

'If that's what he did, his behaviour is regrettable but understandable.'

In all these cases, the speaker signals a contrast between two circumstances. The fact that they are not (unconditionally) asserted to obtain does not present any difficulty: I can signal that possible situations, no less than actual ones, contrast with one another. What this suggests is that it is a mistake to say, as Jackson does, that 'but' is governed by a special rule of assertibility. If the meaning of 'If . . . then . . .' *is* governed by a rule of assertibility, the analogy between 'if' and 'but' cannot be all that close. A uniform meaning-rule can be given for all uses of 'but' whether the sentence that it occurs in is asserted or unasserted.

I propose to consider four types of case in which a conditional is embedded in a longer sentence; also the problems raised by conditionals with disjunctive antecedents mentioned in Section 3.

First, conditional consequents. It seems that 'If P, then if Q then R' is equivalent to 'If P and Q, then R'. (They are of course equivalent if taken just as material conditionals.) But some explanation is needed of the equivalence with a view like Jackson's. Take:

> 'If my information is correct, if he was born in Italy, he left by the time he was three.'

That seems to be assertible in precisely the same conditions as:

> 'If my information is correct and he was born in Italy, he left by the time he was three.'

That can readily be explained if we suppose that the function of 'if' is to signal the assertion of the consequent conditionally upon the truth of the antecedent; for it will be natural (using the notation introduced earlier) to understand an iterated conditional of the form 'If P, then if Q, then R' as signalling the assertion of $\vdash_Q R$ conditionally upon P; and that will be equivalent to $\vdash_{P\&Q} R$. Thus, these cases leave open whether Simple Conditionals have truth-values; but they suggest that Jackson's robustness condition may best be seen as deriving from the role of 'If' to signal a conditional assertion.

The problem with conditionals with disjunctive antecedents is this: 'If P or Q, then R', of course, treated as a material conditional, entails both 'If P then R' and 'If Q then R'. But Adams's hypothesis would mean that 'If P or Q, then R' may be assertible when only one of those truth-functionally entailed consequences is. In fact, however, we are normally ready to assert such a conditional only when we are ready to assert *both* of those conditionals. This suggests that it is not a sufficient condition for the assertibility of something of the form 'If P or Q, then R' that R should be probable relative to the truth of the disjunctive antecedent.

Suppose that,

> 'If John is in Italy or France, he is in Rome'

would be assertible, according to Adams's Hypothesis, if, in fact, if the disjunction in the antecedent is true, it almost certainly is so because John is in Rome; but evidently

'If John is in France, he is in Rome'

is not assertible, and it seems that the original conditional is dubiously assertible precisely because it is not.

A pragmatic explanation of its non-assertibility can be given. If, as we suggested in Section 4, it is misleading to assert 'Either P or Q' solely on the grounds of the truth of one of the disjuncts (especially if there are not reasons for holding that, if that disjunct had been false, the other would have been true) it is understandable why 'If P or Q, then R' should not be assertible when the corresponding conditional probability is attributable to the conditional probability of R given P.

It is a striking fact that disjunctions of conditionals do not seem to have the force that one might have expected them to have from their surface form. If I say,

'Either he will stay in America if he is offered tenure or he will return to Europe if he isn't,'

with the disjoined conditionals taken as material conditionals, that is in fact of the form

[P ⊃ Q] or [not-P ⊃ R]

which is actually tautological. But in fact, such a statement entails the disjunction of its two consequents: it entails that either he will stay in America or he will return to Europe. In that example, the two antecedents exhaust the possibilities because they are contradictories, but that is not true in general. Consider:

'Either she left in disgust, if she found no one there, or she never came in the first place, if the letter changing the date never reached her.'

Here the speaker is saying that either she came and found no one there, or the letter changing the date never reached her and she never came; in the case of each of these two alternatives, if the first thing happened, so did the second.

I think that we can explain the conditions in which such

conditionals are asserted if we suppose that what is said by such disjunction of conditionals might be represented as of the form

Either Q [if P then Q] or S [if R then S].

What is asserted is the disjunction of the two consequents. If we then suppose that the 'If' clause serves to signal conditional assertion, we may suppose that a speaker asserts the disjunction, and, while doing so, indicates a readiness to assert *each* disjunct conditionally. The disjunctive conditional

'Either he is in Rome, if he is in Italy, or he is in Bordeaux, if he is in France'

may be seen as a telescoped version of

'Either he is in Rome or he is in Bordeaux; if he is in Italy he is in Rome; if he is in France he is in Bordeaux.'

It is conditionals with conditional antecedents, and negations of conditionals, that present the greatest problems. First, on the assumption that conditionals have truth-conditions and truth-values, according to the Jackson account, a conditional is assertible just in case its truth is robust with respect to the truth of its antecedent. But, if the antecedent's truth-conditions are those of the material conditional, a sufficient condition of its truth will be the falsehood of the antecedent. On the alternative considered, they will be asserted conditionally upon the antecedent's truth. So, if the conditional in the antecedent is likely to be true in virtue of its antecedent's falsehood, the compound conditional will be assertible if its consequent is probable given the falsehood of the antecedent of the embedded conditional. That does not match the actual assertibility-conditions of such conditionals.

If being over 65 does not entitle you to a reduction,

'If you are over 65, you are entitled to a reduction'

will be true if and only if you are not over 65. It follows that, in those circumstances,

'If you are entitled to a reduction if you are over 65, you were charged too much'

ought, on the view now being considered, to be assertible according to the probability of your having been overcharged on the condition that you are not over 65. But that is plainly not a correct account of the assertibility of the compound conditional.

Worse still, some such compound conditionals would be assertible but false if they are assigned the truth-conditions of the material conditional. Gibbard gives the following example:[4]

'If the cup broke if it was dropped, it was fragile.'

With the truth-conditions of the material conditional, that will be false if the cup was not dropped and was not fragile, but in fact it may well be assertible under those conditions.

It seems hard to resist the conclusion that the 'if'-clause in such a case specifies a hypothesis that we can consider as being either so or not so (and therefore, if Dummett's suggestion is correct, true or false). But it appears that the hypothesis in question when we have a conditional antecedent is not the truth of the corresponding material conditional. The example just given suggests that the hypothesis in question is that some condition is fulfilled that would, in the circumstances, have made the antecedent conditional assertible on its own. In the example, it would be that the cup was disposed, in the circumstances, to break if dropped; such a disposition would support the consequent 'it was fragile' if the disposition was attributable to the character of the cup, and not, for example, the height at which the cup was held.

Likewise,

'If you are over 65, you are entitled to a reduction'

is assertible or not on the basis of the relevant regulations, and that is the hypothesis expressed in:

'If you are entitled to a reduction if you are over 65, you were charged too much.'

This suggests that it is misguided to attribute to Simple Conditionals the truth-conditions of the material conditional. As we have seen, such a theory has to hold that some conditionals are false that are actually assertible. This does not fit well with the thesis that the meaning of 'if' imposes a further condition beyond the condition that what is asserted be true, assuming that the truth-conditions are those of the material conditional.

---

[4] 'Two Recent Theories of Conditionals', 237.

A theory that holds that Simple Conditionals lack truth-values, when asserted on their own, is in a better position to account for their behaviour when they occur as the antecedents of complex conditionals; for, even if it has to be conceded that, occurring thus, they express something that is so or not (and therefore true or false), *what* they express can be seen as derivative from their non-truth-valued use, standing on their own. As we saw, the hypothesis introduced by a conditional 'If'-clause can be that some condition, to be gathered from the context, is fulfilled that would support the corresponding conditional assertion.[5]

Finally, as an alternative, we can hold that Simple Conditionals *do* have truth-conditions, but not those of the material conditional: what is asserted to be the case by 'If P then Q' is precisely what, in the context, would be hypothesized to be so, in the context, by 'If, if P then Q, then . . .'. As we have seen, in view of Lewis's result, the truth-conditions of Simple Conditionals will be highly context-relative, and relative, in particular, to the speaker's state of knowledge.

Many of the same problems recur when we consider negations of conditionals. The obvious difficulty with a theory that assigns them the truth-conditions of the material conditional is that 'It is not the case that if P then Q' will be equivalent to 'P and not-Q'. But there seems to be no way of hearing

> 'It's not true that if Jones was at the meeting, he voted for the proposal'

as saying that Jones was present and did not vote for it. We do describe conditionals as true or false; but when one is described as not true, the person thus describing it is not taken to have asserted the conjunction of the antecedent and the negation of the consequent.

Now in fact, if we consider the example just mentioned:

> 'It's not true that if Jones was at the meeting he voted for the proposal,'

---

[5] See Mackie, *Truth, Probability, and Paradox*, 103 and Gibbard, 'Two Recent Theories of Conditionals', 238.

we can fairly easily see one way of understanding it. It is easily taken as saying:

> 'If Jones was at the meeting, it's not true that he voted for the proposal (i.e. he didn't vote for it).'

In general, 'It's not true that if P then Q' is typically taken as equivalent to 'If P, it's not true that Q'. If we take this line, an explanation is needed, not of the fact that a sentence of that form is susceptible of that interpretation, but that the other interpretation, giving the negation wide scope, is not available.

An explanation *is* available, if we understand Simple Conditionals as conditional assertions. For this explanation makes the conditional clause in a certain sense subordinate, as is suggested by grammar. Thus, an explanation is available of the fact that negation is typically taken as operating on the consequent. It will be available to those who, whether or not they ascribe Simple Conditionals material truth-conditions, view them as conditional assertions.

Unfortunately, this explanation will not cover all cases. If someone says,

> 'If you are over 65, you are entitled to a reduction,'

and is met with the response 'That's not true', the remark will certainly *not* be taken as saying that you are over 65 and not entitled to a reduction; but equally, it *need* not be taken as the denial of the consequent conditionally upon the truth of the antecedent. It is naturally taken as denying that being over 65 guarantees a reduction.

If what has been said about conditionals with conditional antecedents is correct, there is an explanation if Simple Conditionals, uttered on their own, are taken as conditional assertions, lacking a truth-value. We can say that the negation of a Simple Conditional is often treated as the denial of the condition that, in the context, would have made the Simple Conditional assertible; in the example, that the regulations allow a reduction to those over that age.[6]

---

[6] In fact, Grice, who attempted to explain the restrictions on the use of 'If P then Q' pragmatically, recognized that the denials of conditionals posed serious problems for his theory.

Something may be done to dispel any suggestion that this account is *ad hoc* if we note that the response 'That's not true' to 'He certainly travelled to Siena' may be taken either as a denial that he travelled to Siena, or as a denial that the conditions for a confident assertion that he did so (marked by 'certainly') are fulfilled.

In this section, I have argued that the theory that makes Simple Conditionals equivalent in their truth-conditions to material conditionals must be rejected. I have also argued that a conditional-assertion theory, that regards them as lacking truth-values, can explain their behaviour when embedded in longer sentences.

# 7

# A Theory of Simple Conditionals; Non-Assertoric Conditionals

If possible worlds theories, and the theory that the truth-conditions of Simple Conditionals are those of the material conditional are rejected, we are left, first, with the view that Simple Conditionals are to be explained as being used to make conditional assertions, so that they do not express propositions to which a truth-value may be ascribed (though a truth-value may be assigned to the consequent in the event of the antecedent's truth); and second the view that such conditionals do have truth-conditions of a relativized kind—relativized to the epistemic state of the speaker. How should we decide between these alternatives?

The general question of what justifies the ascription of a truth-value to utterances made using a particular form of words raises general issues. But here, I will consider some arguments offered recently by Dorothy Edgington, who develops a powerful case for the position that (Simple) conditionals *cannot* be given truth-conditions. Other writers have argued along similar lines.[1]

Against the view that Simple Conditionals have the truth-conditions of the material conditional, Edgington argues that *believing* a conditional cannot be identified with believing that those truth-conditions are fulfilled. Her argument takes the form of a dilemma: if Simple Conditionals have truth-conditions, they are either those of the material conditional or not; but either alternative has unacceptable consequences. One argument against the first hypothesis is that, quite generally, believing that P can be no more than believing that P's truth-conditions are fulfilled. She writes (p. 186):

There is simply no evidence that one *believes* a conditional whenever one

---

[1] See 'Do Conditionals Have Truth-Conditions?', *Crítica*, 18, No. 52 (1986), 3–30, reprinted in Jackson (ed.), *Conditionals*, 176–201; see esp. pp. 188–97. Page references in what follows are to the Jackson edition.

believes the corresponding material implication, and then is prepared to *assert* it only when some further condition is satisfied.

This argument can be seen as different from, but parallel to, the argument of the last section about the behaviour of 'If P then Q', when it occurs within the scope of a truth-functional connective. Just as one who denies 'If P then Q' does not deny the fulfilment of the material truth-conditions, so it is not right to say that in believing that 'If P then Q', we merely believe the truth-conditions are fulfilled. But some account must be given of what it is to believe a conditional, something that is not fixed by specifying their assertibility-conditions, or saying that they are used to make conditional assertions. We need to make sense of an occurrence of 'If P then Q' after 'A believes that . . .'; and the question arises whether that can be done without ascribing truth-conditions.

This is related to a difficulty raised by Edgington when she asks (p. 186) what theoretical purpose is served by ascribing truth-conditions to them. Our intuitions no doubt favour such ascriptions (we say, for example 'It is true that if John was there, no one remarked on the fact') but they hardly favour the ascription of those of the material conditional. So it seems that the issue needs to be decided on general theoretical grounds.[2]

Edgington offers an explanation of what it is to believe a Simple Conditional: she says (p. 188), 'X believes that (judges it likely that) if A, B, to the extent that he judges that A & B is nearly as likely as A'; which, of course, is the same thing as judging that the relevant conditional probability is high.

The question then arises whether, on that account, belief in a conditional is not a belief that something is the case, as we saw with other embedded conditionals in the last section. That Q is probable, given P, is something that is so or not, given an assignment of probabilities.

Edgington tries to dispose of the other horn of her dilemma—

---

[2] A second argument of Edgington's is that, if conditionals have truth-conditions, 'to judge it more or less probable that if A, B, is to judge it more or less probable that its truth-conditions obtain'. But that simply begs the question against the view that, in the case of Simple Conditionals, probability is not simply probability of truth. Still, the separation of these has been thought by some so hard to accept that, as we saw earlier, the combination of Lewis and Adams has been thought to force the conclusion that Simple Conditionals lack truth-conditions.

that Simple Conditionals have non-material truth-conditions—
by arguing that any breakdown in truth-functionality would
show up in uncertainty about the truth-value of 'If P then Q' in
the presence of certainty about the truth-values of P and Q. She
rightly argues that one who is certain that P and Q are both true,
or that P is true and Q false, cannot rationally be uncertain
whether to accept 'If P then Q'. She then argues against a breakdown in truth-functionality in the case when the antecedent is
false, on the grounds that one who knows that Q is true and is
totally uncertain about the truth-value of P could not rationally
be uncertain about whether if P then Q. That is clearly the case:
if I am certain that Q, either I regard it as probabilistically independent of P or not. If I do, I shall regard the unconditional
probability of Q as being the same as its probability given P, and
'If P then Q' must be acceptable. If not, I cannot rationally be
*certain* that Q if I am uncertain whether P. The problem is that if
I am certain that Q is true, and also certain that P is false, I may
or may not be ready to accept 'If P then Q'. Such certainties are
consistent with the conditional probability of Q given P being
either high or low. As we saw earlier, I may be certain that I am
at the site of a Roman encampment and that my evidence for this
is reliable, without accepting that if, contrary to what I believe,
the evidence is *un*reliable, there was a Roman encampment here.[3]

So the possibility of assigning Simple Conditionals non-truth-
functional truth-conditions still stands, provided that we accept
the degree of relativization that is required. It may be thought
that, if Simple Conditionals have to be assigned truth-conditions

---

[3] [Woods makes a slip here: if one is certain that P is false, one's conditional
probability for Q given P does not exist. The argument of Edgington's under discussion does not rest on this case. As Woods notes, she considers the case of certainty that Q combined with uncertainty about P; and Woods agrees with her that
this is sufficient for certainty that if P, Q. But with truth-conditions which allow
the conditional to be false when P is false and Q is true, this epistemic state would
not be sufficient for certainty that if P, Q, because for all you know, it may be the
case that P is false, Q is true, and 'If P then Q' is false. Hence it is an argument
against such truth-conditions.

Woods's example of the Roman encampment can be construed thus. I am, to
all intents and purposes, certain that I am at the site of a Roman encampment.
However, when I say 'If the evidence is unreliable . . .' I am taking this antecedent
as an epistemic possibility, as not certainly false, however unlikely. Then he is
right to say that I do not accept that there was a Roman encampment here, under
this hypothesis.]

when they occur embedded in a longer sentence, we have a more straightforward theory if they have the same truth-conditions when uttered on their own. However, problems arise with iterated conditionals. The suggestion is that 'If P then Q' is true if and only if the probability of Q given P is high, relative to the speaker's epistemic state.[4] But if we take a conditional of the form 'If P, then if Q then R', it seems that the conditional in the consequent has to be evaluated as true relative not to the speaker's *actual* epistemic state, but one which is conditional on P's being the case. Thus,

> 'If the building is a listed building, then if they altered the fireplace, they acted illegally'

will be true according to the probability of the truth of the consequent conditionally on the truth of the antecedent, with the consequent's truth determined by the epistemic state that the speaker would be in if the antecedent were known to be true. In fact, on such a theory, not merely the truth-value, but also the truth-conditions of a conditional consequent will depend on the antecedent. Moreover, it is then hard to explain why 'If P, then if Q then R' should always be equivalent to 'If P and Q, then R' as we saw they were in the last section.[5]

---

[4] [Woods's observation that Edgington has not ruled out truth-conditions for conditionals which are relative to a speaker's epistemic state is correct. (She sets aside this possibility on p. 194.) But the suggestion he canvasses here is not the best one. A better suggestion would be that given the speaker's epistemic state, we can find a proposition the probability of whose truth is matched by the conditional probability of consequent given antecedent. It is not a good proposal that the context-relative proposition be *true* (as opposed to probable) when the speaker has a high conditional probability for consequent given antecedent, for the following reasons. (i) Suppose that in a given context, a speaker has a conditional probability of Q given P of 99 per cent, and this counts as high. Then according to the proposal, the truth-condition for the conditional is satisfied, the speaker knows that it is satisfied, and the speaker should be certain that the conditional is true. But the speaker is not certain that if P then Q. There is the added disadvantage that the truth of 'If P then Q' is compatible with 'P and not Q'. (ii) Suppose that a speaker has a conditional probability of Q given P of 50 per cent, and this does not count as high. The truth-condition is not satisfied, the speaker knows this, and should be certain that the conditional is not true: should assign probability zero to 'If P then Q'. But the speaker thinks it is 50–50 that if P then Q.]

[5] For this argument that, with the theory that ascribes truth-conditions to Simple Conditionals, there will be no epistemic state by reference to which the embedded conditional can be evaluated, I am indebted to Allan Gibbard in 'Two Theories of Conditionals', 234–5. He shows that, given the equivalence of 'If P,

It seems, then, that the view that Simple Conditionals have non-truth-functional, epistemically relativized, truth-conditions leads only to greater complexity, and we can more readily account for the phenomena if we treat an utterance of conditional form as a conditional assertion, while allowing that embedded conditionals can be treated as true or false. Are there any residual reasons for wanting to ascribe truth-conditions to unembedded conditionals?

Doubts may be felt about assigning only assertibility-conditions to 'If P then Q', since Q may prove false even if the conditional probability of Q given P is high; yet one who asserts 'If P then Q' is shown to be wrong if it turns out that P is true and Q false, irrespective of the prior conditional probability.[6] But this is not an objection to the conditional assertion view; on the account defended, one who asserts 'If P then Q' is committed to the truth of Q in the event of P's being true, even though the grounds for making the conditional assertion are grounds for the relevant conditional probability.

On this view, it is easy to see why 'If P then Q' and 'If P then not-Q' are not jointly assertible by a single speaker; and why, if each is uttered by different persons, one of the two assertions is false if P is in fact true; why if P is not true, both utterances may be well-founded, given different, and not necessarily conflicting, evidence. If Jones was not present at the meeting, there is no conflict between one person's evidence that everyone present voted for the proposal and another's that, Jones's character and opinions being what they were, he would never have voted for it.[7]

Someone who sincerely asserts 'If P then Q' expresses a conditional belief in the truth of the consequent—a conditional acceptance of it. This state is characterized by sensitivity to

then if Q, then R' to 'If P and Q, then R', if the proposition expressed by 'If P then Q' is fixed in a uniform way as a function of P and Q and the speaker's epistemic state, 'If P then Q' *has* to be taken as equivalent to the material conditional, an option that we have rejected. The example in the text illustrates the fact that, with relativized non-truth-functional truth-conditions, in 'If P, then if Q then R', the proposition expressed by 'If Q then R' cannot be determined independently of P.

[6] See Bennett, 'Farewell to the Phlogiston Theory of Conditionals', 509–27; and V. H. Dudman, 'Appiah on "If"', *Analysis*, 47 (1987), 74–9.

[7] Compare the Mississippi riverboat example, Gibbard, 'Two Recent Theories of Conditionals', 226–7, cited in Section 3 above, p. 28.

evidence bearing on the relevant conditional probability. Such a belief, though not manifested in the way that an unconditional belief would be, may be manifested in other ways—for example, typically in readiness to accept the consequent unconditionally if the truth of the antecedent is learned, and a readiness to take account of the possibility of the consequent's truth to the extent that it is thought that the antecedent may be true. Similarly, a conditional belief may be communicated by the utterance of a Simple Conditional; or an unconditional belief may be communicated to someone who already accepts the truth of the antecedent.

It seems that a hearer has fully grasped the purport of an utterance of 'If P then Q' when he recognizes what is being conditionally asserted, and on what condition. But the conditional assertion, if well-founded, will rest on certain unconditional beliefs of the speaker, and, in many cases, it will be contextually evident what those beliefs are. For example, it will normally be evident what beliefs ground an utterance of

'If you are over 65, you are entitled to a reduction.'

It seems that such grounding beliefs make it possible to take Simple Conditionals, when they occur embedded in a longer sentence, as expressing something that can be assigned a truth-value.

Thus someone who denies

'If this church is Romanesque, it was built before 1250'

is naturally taken as denying that all Romanesque churches were built before 1250. Someone who denies

'If you reduce your intake of salt, your blood pressure will decrease'

will presumably be denying the existence of a certain causal connection.

Given the numerous occasions on which we should be ready to assert one thing conditionally on something else, and given that we have beliefs that are conditional in the sense explained, it would indeed be surprising if we lacked the linguistic means for making conditional assertions. The view defended here makes assertoric conditionals nicely parallel to conditional commands and questions, to which we now turn.

What, then, should be said about conditional commands and conditional questions? In the case of commands, it might be thought that a distinction could be drawn between a conditional command and a command whose obedience-conditions are specified conditionally. One might expect that, corresponding to a conditional in the indicative mood in the second person singular, there will be a transformation of that sentence into the imperative mood; and that the imperative would have, for its obedience-conditions, the fulfilment of the truth-conditions of the indicative. We have seen that there are reasons for ascribing truth-conditions to embedded conditionals.

Equally, though, we might think that there are or could be conditional commands of a different sort. We could suppose that someone could issue a command that was conditional in the sense that whether any command was given at all depended on whether something was the case; if it was not, no command was given at all.[8]

Given what I have said earlier in this section about the meaning of the 'If . . . then . . .' form of words and the notion of conditional assertion, we might expect that a sentence in which the imperative mood occurs along with an 'If'-clause would be especially apt for the making of conditional commands: just as I have argued that 'If P then Q' is used to assert that Q on the condition that P, we might think that 'If P, then do X' commands X conditionally on P's being the case.

But the question now arises what the connection is between these two suggestions. Are there in fact two ways of taking an utterance of the 'If P, then bring it about that Q' form—one as a command to bring it about that Q on the condition that P is the case, and the other as an unconditional command to bring about the truth of 'If P then Q', assigned truth-conditions in the same way as other embedded conditionals? In fact, it seems that there is no room for a distinction here: we cannot really distinguish between an understanding of 'If John calls, tell him that I have gone out' that takes it as requiring the person to give this

---

[8] We may follow Dummett in comparing conditional commands with conditional bets (like a bet that if a certain party wins the next election, a certain person remains as the leader of it). If the party does not win, it is as if no bet had been made at all. See Dummett, 'Truth', repr. in *Truth and Other Enigmas*, 9.

information to John on condition that he calls, and taking it to prescribe to the person addressed that he make it true that John does not call without being told that I have gone out. It seems best to take all utterances of the form 'If P, then do X' as conditional commands.

Matters seem to be different with conditional questions. If I am asked,

'If John is over 60, is he entitled to a rail card?'

it is not a conditional question in the sense that, if John is not over 60, the asking of the question lapses. Someone to whom that was addressed would be expected to respond with a reply irrespective of the fulfilment of the antecedent; and an affirmative response to it would be taken as counting as an assertion of a conditional form.

With that may be contrasted,

'If you were born before 1940, have you qualified for a pension?'

where the question is asked only conditionally on the obtaining of a certain circumstance. The reply, if the question of reply arises at all, would not be of a conditional form.

The examples given so far have been of sentential questions, but a similar distinction can be drawn for questions of the other sort. Compare

'If he escaped, how did he do so?'

with

'If you are the person in charge, what do you propose to do about the present situation?'

What we need to recognize in the case of questions is a contrast between the attaching of an 'If'-clause to a sentence already of interrogative form, and the transformation of a conditional in the indicative into a question whose content has a conditional form. Here, once again, we need to appeal to the theory of embedded conditionals already outlined. 'Is it the case that if P then Q?' expresses an enquiry into the fulfilment of certain truth-conditions, truth-conditions that are derivative, in the way suggested, from the use of a conditional, on its own, to make a conditional assertion. With that should be contrasted the question 'If P, is it the case that Q?', where that asks a question upon a certain condition.[9]

[9] [Woods here indicated that he intended to complete the present section with a discussion of 'even if' and 'only if'.]

# 8

# Sketch of a Theory
# of 'Counterfactual' Conditionals

In Section 2, I argued that the Counterfactuality Thesis is false; and in Section 5, I argued against the attempt to explain 'counterfactual' conditionals in terms of possible worlds. Having, in the last section, developed an account of the meaning of 'if' when it occurs in Simple Conditionals, it remains to sketch a theory of 'counterfactuals' that meets the requirements identified in Section 5. So I begin by returning to the question of the logical form of conditionals employing 'would'.

There is a class of sentences that have normally been classified along with what I have been calling Simple Conditionals, under the influence, undoubtedly, of the Counterfactuality Thesis.[1] Take an example like:

'If it rains this afternoon the match will be cancelled.'

This clearly has no counterfactual implications. It seems reasonable to say that neither does:

'If it were to rain this afternoon, the match would be cancelled,'

though perhaps the latter carries, as the former does not, the suggestion that the antecedent is unlikely to be fulfilled.

If we reject the Counterfactuality Thesis, as I have argued we should, for such conditionals as:

---

[1] Here I need to acknowledge a debt to Vic Dudman. My dogmatic slumbers on the subject of so-called counterfactual conditionals, though not first disturbed, were fully dispelled by the work of Dudman, particularly 'Conditional Interpretations of "If"-Sentences', *Australian Journal of Linguistics*, 4 (1984), 143–204. Much of what Dudman says seems to me to be certainly correct, though I have reservations about other things. What I want to do is to offer more of an account of the purport of those conditionals that have been classified as counterfactual than Dudman attempts to do.

'If he came now, he would be very surprised,'

then the way is open for us to adopt the very natural view that this reports precisely what would have been reported by someone who uttered,

'If he comes tomorrow he will be very surprised,'

yesterday.

In other words, we may take the sentence containing 'would' as a past tense version of the one containing 'will'. If we take that position, it is already clear that a 'would'- sentence like

'If it had rained yesterday afternoon, the match would have been cancelled'

is not straightforwardly of the 'If . . . then . . .' form, involving as it does the application of a past tense to something already of conditional form. As we saw in Section 2, it is not constructed from two sentences, each independently past-tensed, by applying the 'If . . . then . . .' construction to them.[2] But should we take the same view about:

'If it rains this afternoon, the match will be cancelled'?

Should we regard it as not straightforwardly of the 'If . . . then . . .' form?

We have the present tense in the 'If'-clause (though the main clause seems to have the future tense, as indicated by 'will'); but this occurrence of the present in the 'If'-clause is held to be simply an idiosyncrasy of English. That is the standard view. So it is suggested that the purport of:

'If it rains this afternoon, the match will be cancelled,'

would be more perspicuously conveyed by:

'If it will rain this afternoon, the match will be cancelled.'

We can then, it is alleged, see that what we have is two sentences combined with 'If . . . then . . .' both of which concern the future. So what we have *is*, really, of the 'If . . . then . . .' form, involving the application of 'If . . . then . . .' to a pair of sentences.

---

[2] It follows, as Dudman points out, that we have really no business speaking of the antecedent and consequent in a case like this.

It is now possible to see, without begging any questions, that this cannot be a correct account of the matter. If the presence of the grammatical present tense in:

'If it rains, the match will be cancelled,'

is simply a quirk of English, we should expect that the sentence that I just produced, with 'will rain' substituted for 'rains' should be either ungrammatical (which it plainly is not) or else an optional equivalent for the one with the present tense; and that is clearly not so either. One difference is that the 'if it rains' version implies, as the 'if it will rain' version does not, that the cancellation occurs *after* the occurrence of rain. Roughly, one sentence predicts cancellation in the event of its raining; the other predicts cancellation, conditionally on something's being the case, namely that it is going to rain.[3]

If the natural view is taken that the 'would' sentence is a past-tense version of the 'will' sentence, we can see that it is a great distortion to concentrate attention on sentences containing 'would', as those who have elaborated theories of 'counterfactual' conditionals have done. It is rather like focusing attention on statements of the form 'Jones believed that P' when discussing the logical form of attributions of propositional attitudes.

If we compare:

'If it rains, the match will be cancelled,'

with:

'If it had rained, the match would have been cancelled,'

or:

'If it rained, the match would be cancelled,'

we note that, in addition to the change from 'will' to 'would', we have 'rains' replaced by 'rained' or 'had rained', and sometimes

---

[3] We may also note the difference between:

'If she will see the letter when she comes in, you had better tell her it's from an old school friend,'

and

'If she sees the letter when she comes in, you had better tell her it's from an old school friend.'

also the replacement of 'will be' by 'would have been'. It has commonly been held that, just as the 'will'-conditional is about the future, with the occurrence of 'will' indicating that fact, the others are about the past, or possibly the present, and that the tense of the verb indicates this.

But what is the significance of the tenses? As we saw earlier, it is clear that it is not signifying the time of the fulfilment of the antecedent. We can have:

> 'If it had rained tomorrow afternoon, the match would have been cancelled,'

just as we can have:

> 'If you came next Thursday, you would have been very surprised.'

Any theory of conditionals needs to have an explanation of the difference between:

(1) If he comes tomorrow, he will be very surprised;

(2) If he came tomorrow, he would be very surprised;

(3) If he had come tomorrow, he would have been very surprised;

and, in particular, of the difference in tenses—an explanation that does not wrongly claim that they signify the time of the fulfilment or non-fulfilment, as the case may be, of something specified in the 'If'-clause.

If my general approach is correct, we need to concentrate our attention first on conditional 'will'-statements like:

> 'If he catches the train, he will arrive on time.'

In fact, the 'will' is firmly present-tensed, and what is described is something about the present, even though it has implications concerning the future.

What is the logical form of such sentences? I suggest that they are best understood as containing an application of the present-tense 'will' to a sentence or predicate that is already of the 'If . . . then . . .' form. If so, the final sentence will not itself be of that form. The 'If . . . then . . .' construction is the same, semantically, as the one that we find in sentences of the 'If . . . then . . .' form built up from two arbitrary sentences, but we have to regard the 'If . . . then . . .' as having been introduced at an earlier stage in the construction of the sentence in the case of:

> 'If John catches the train, he will arrive in time,'

than it was in the case of:

> 'If John caught the train, he arrived in time.'

We should see the first of those sentences as built up in the following way. Take first the two sentences,

> 'John catches the train,'

and

> 'John arrives in time,'

thought of as lacking significant tensing. We can apply the 'If . . . then . . .' construction to them, so that we get:

> 'If John catches the train, John arrives in time.'

We can then think of 'will' as being applied to the whole sentence, so as to yield something which might be represented as:

> 'Will (If John catches the train, John arrives in time),'

or, more intelligibly:

> 'It will be the case that, if John catches the train, he arrives in time.'

This appears in natural English as:

> 'If John catches the train, he will arrive in time,'

in which 'will' is present-tensed, and governs the whole sentence.

I claim that the 'will', though it occurs as an auxiliary forming the main verb in the apodosis, in fact has as its scope a sentence, or at least a predicate, so that it has wider scope than the grammatical 'If' clause.[4] If 'will' is treated as a modal expression, we

---

[4] Dudman in fact argues that, in such cases, 'will' always serves to form a complex conditional predicate, so that, for example,

> 'If we run out of beer, James will go out and buy some more'

is to be taken as, in effect,

should not be surprised that, although it occurs grammatically as part of the apodosis of the 'If . . . then . . .' sentence, its scope is the whole conditional. Exactly the same phenomenon occurs with the modal expression 'necessarily' in:

> 'If Peter has a driver's licence, he is necessarily over seventeen.'

Likewise, 'certainly' in:

> 'If Mary came to the party, she certainly left early.'

So much, then, for the logical form of the sentence under discussion. How, exactly, is 'will' to be understood when it operates on a sentence or predicate itself of conditional form?

We may make use of the theory of embedded conditionals and their truth-values developed in the last two sections to understand the embedding of a conditional sentence with the operator 'It will be the case that'. I suggest that the purport of 'It will be the case that if P then Q' or, more familiarly, 'If P, it will be the case that Q', is something like the following: 'Matters are (now) such as to ground an assertion of "If P then Q", where this is a matter of the *objective* probability of Q, given P: what would be assertible from an ideal epistemic standpoint.'[5] If we wanted to sum up what is reported in the present by 'will', and in the past by 'would', we could say it is the presence of a tendency or disposition. If it is true that if it rains the match will be cancelled, matters are so disposed as to ensure cancellation in the event of rain. But exactly *what* is reported by 'will' will vary as much from case to case as the circumstances in which a Simple Conditional is assertible, as we saw in the last section.

---

> 'James will: get-some-more-beer-if-we-run-out.'

In such a case, it seems to make no difference whether we take 'James' as being inside the scope of 'will' (names are scopeless). But if the position in the sentence occupied by 'James' is replaced by a quantifier, there is room for alternative readings, depending on the scope of 'will'. Take:

> 'If we run out of beer, someone will go out and buy some more.'

So Dudman seems to be wrong in holding that 'will' always serves as a predicate-forming operator.

[5] This is not intended as an analysis, but an informal representation of the content of a sentence in which a conditional occurs within the scope of the 'will' operator.

We saw earlier that Simple Conditionals are properly understood *epistemically*: whether 'If P then Q' is acceptable is a matter of the conditional probability of Q, given P. I have now argued that a sentence of the form 'If P is the case, Q will be the case' is best not understood as a Simple Conditional.

The effect of putting the conditional within the scope of 'will' is to de-relativize the judgement, so that its assertibility turns on the *objective* probability of Q, given P, and not on the speaker's subjective epistemic position. The full defence of this depends on whether I am correct about the relationship between 'will' judgements and 'would' judgements.[6]

The hypothesis is that 'If P were the case, Q would be the case' is true if and only if at some earlier date (to be gathered from the context) 'If P is the case, Q will be the case' was assertible, and that this is so even if P and Q concern the present or the future. Support may be provided for the hypothesis if we return to the cases with which we began, of the contrast between Simple and 'counterfactual' conditionals concerning the past, when a Simple Conditional is assertible, but the corresponding 'counterfactual' conditional would not be.

In the Kennedy example, given the epistemic state that someone is in after the event, knowing that *someone* assassinated Kennedy, they would be ready to say:

'If Oswald did not assassinate Kennedy, someone else did.'

What, then, about:

'If Kennedy had not been assassinated by Oswald, someone else would have assassinated him'?

According to the hypothesis I am defending, that should be acceptable if, at some appropriate time in the past,

'If Oswald does not assassinate Kennedy, someone else will do so'

was acceptable—acceptable, that is, from the standpoint of some-

---

[6] A view along these lines has been put forward by Ernest Adams and Brian Skyrms, but it has not enjoyed the vogue it deserves, in face of the high tide of possible-worlds theories. See Adams, *The Logic of Conditionals*, ch. 4; B. Skyrms, 'The Prior Propensity Account of Subjunctive Conditionals', in Harper, Stalnaker, and Pearce (eds.), *Ifs*, 259–65.

one who is apprised of all the relevant facts about how things are up to the time when the forward-looking conditional is asserted. We are not envisaging an *actual* epistemic point of view—a state of knowledge that someone might actually have been in antecedently; rather, we are describing things from an *ideal* epistemic perspective.

We get a similar result in a case in which, instead, a 'counterfactual' conditional is regarded as being well supported, but the corresponding Simple Conditional is not. Speaking about a lottery, I may say:

> 'If I had (had had) the winning ticket, I would now be (have been) rich,'

but not:

> 'If I had the winning ticket, I am now rich.'[7]

I know that I am not now rich, and, under the supposition that I have the winning ticket, I do not then envisage myself as changing my opinion about my wealth. Instead, I would now say:

> 'If I have the winning ticket, I have been defrauded, or the lottery was mismanaged.'

But, as things are, I do not believe that there has been any fraud or mismanagement; and therefore I *am* prepared to say that if I had had the winning ticket, I would now be rich. I am suggesting that this is because, from the point of view of someone *before* the lottery was decided, who had access to all the relevant information, it would have been appropriate to say, 'If I have the winning ticket, I shall be rich.'

Evidence in favour of this suggestion is provided by examples that have been held to show that the Ramsey test is inapplicable to some conditionals. The Kennedy example shows that it does not fit retrospective 'counterfactuals'—those concerning some past situation—because there would then be no difference in the acceptability-conditions of 'counterfactuals' and the corresponding Simple Conditionals. But there are difficulties for the Ramsey Test as an account of certain conditionals referring to the future. So if, as I have been arguing, 'will'-conditionals are not Simple

---

[7] I owe this example to Frank Jackson in *Conditionals*, 71.

Conditionals at all, the fact that the Ramsey Test doesn't work for them is not an argument against it.

The relevant cases are those in which the discovery of the truth of the antecedent would give strong grounds for the acceptability of a conditional, but, in the absence of such knowledge of its truth, the conditional in question would not be acceptable. It follows from this that the conditional probability of Q given P is high, so the conditional ought to be acceptable anyway by the Ramsey Test; but in fact the conditional is not supported in the absence of evidence provided by the antecedent's truth.

To illustrate, we may suppose that the question arises whether Jones will apply for a certain job, and whether, if he applies, he will be successful. I may know that Jones would not apply without some encouragement to do so, from those offering it; and we may also suppose that they will not encourage anyone to apply unless they are virtually certain to offer the appointment to them if they do so. In these circumstances, if I learn that Jones has applied, I will assign a high probability to his getting it; but I need not, *in advance*, accept that if he were to apply, he would have a strong chance of getting it; so the conditional is not acceptable merely on the strength of passing the Ramsey Test. Nor, equally, will I say 'If he applies, he will have a strong chance of getting the position'; so *that* conditional, too, is not judged acceptable or not according to whether it passes the Ramsey Test. In order to be justified in asserting either of these forward-looking conditionals, I should need to have relevant information about Jones's qualifications for the post, or about what his qualifications will be perceived to be; and this is a matter of the conditional probability that would be assigned to his getting the position, if he applied, by someone occupying an ideal epistemic position.

If we consider the situation I described retrospectively, we notice that, not knowing whether Jones has applied or not, I might say that if he applied, he had a good chance of getting the job, but not be prepared to say that, if he *had* applied, he would have had a good chance.

Examples like this one seem to confirm the suggestion that conditionals of the form 'If P is the case, Q will be the case' are to be classed along with those that have traditionally been called 'counterfactual'. It also suggests the positive account of their logical form that I have sketched. The sort of information that would justify the assertion, in the first example I gave, of

'If Jones applies, he will very likely get the job,'

are facts about Jones's personal characteristics and how they will be regarded by the organization in question. These facts are of a dispositional sort: they can be specified as those that would ensure Jones's success if he applied. We have to suppose that the relevant time is before Jones's decision whether to apply or not, and also before any decision whether to make him an offer.

I said earlier that any theory of conditionals needs to have an explanation of the difference between:

(1) If he comes tomorrow, he will be very surprised;

(2) If he came tomorrow, he would be very surprised;

(3) If he had come tomorrow, he would have been very surprised;

granted that they may each concern the same future time. I have already outlined what I take to be the proper explanation of (1). I have also indicated that I regard 'would' as being simply the past tense of 'will'; so it is natural to expect that (2) is simply the past-tense version of (1). We need no longer be surprised that (2) concerns the future, nor regard that as counting against the view that 'would' is a past tense, and that the sentence as a whole is used to say something about what was the case at some past time; exactly what past time would be something requiring to be determined contextually. This may be supported by the fact that, if I know the truth of (1), I can claim that knowledge by saying,

'I know that if he comes tomorrow, he will be very surprised,'

and I can later ascribe such knowledge to myself retrospectively by saying that I knew that if he came he would be very surprised.

None the less, an example like (2) may provoke resistance to the idea that (2) is simply (1) transformed into the past tense. After all, it seems to report how things are now just as much as (1) does, and indeed may seem to differ from (1) very little so far as its truth-conditions are concerned. A speaker using (2) instead of (1) might suggest thereby that the fulfilment of the antecedent is a remote possibility, a suggestion not carried by (1).

Despite these appearances, we should regard (2) as about the past, even though a speaker who uses (2) will normally wish to convey something about the present also. Dispositions and tendencies recorded by the use of 'will' and 'would' are typically continuing, sometimes fairly long-term, things; so asserting the existence of such a tendency in the past may, in a context, be taken as compatible with its continuation into the present.

A conditional tendency can no longer be ascribed after the possibility of its exercise has lapsed as a result of the non-fulfilment of the condition.[8] This is of particular significance in those cases in which the time for the fulfilment of the condition is fixed with some degree of precision either by an explicit temporal indication in the 'if'-clause or by the context.

It follows from this that the past tense will be used on those occasions on which the possibility of the fulfilment of the condition for the exercise of the disposition or the tendency has lapsed. This will explain what the effect of using (2) rather than (1) is. It involves a form of words that is appropriate when the existence of a past conditional disposition is being reported, and so suggests that the fulfilment of the condition is in fact remote, even though it is not strictly being implied that the conditional tendency no longer persists.

What, then, should we say about (3)? The most natural response might be that a statement of the form 'If A had been the case, B would have been the case' is simply the past tense version of one of the 'If A has been the case, B will have been the case' form, involving what traditional grammar called the perfect and the future perfect tenses. This is surely the correct thing to say about some statements of the form of (3), but it may be unclear whether it is the correct thing to say about (3) itself. I think there is in fact nothing deviant about:

'If he has come tomorrow, he will have been very surprised,'

---

[8] Thus, there is no question of a disposition for something to be the case conditionally upon Saddam Hussein's having won the Gulf War. This doesn't mean, of course, that we can't ascribe a disposition upon a certain condition; but then the disposition thus ascribed (in general, anyway) is not a conditional disposition, and, if the condition in question is not fulfilled, no disposition is ascribed.

despite the presence of the perfect tense, along with the future time indicator 'tomorrow' in the 'if'-clause. What we need to bear in mind is that the conditional statement, as a whole, is about the present, and what the 'if'-clause specifies is the fulfilment of a condition tomorrow, a condition that consists in something's having already occurred before tomorrow. What the 'will' does is to assert the existence of a tendency that ensured the previous occurrence of the state of affairs described in the consequent.

This, in itself, should not be found paradoxical. There is something essentially general about dispositions and tendencies, and hence a disposition that continues into the present may be what is enough to ensure that one thing has already happened, given that something else has. Thus, we report a present trait of Sadie's character when we say:

> 'If she has taken up hang-gliding, she will have taken out adequate insurance.'[9]

I suggest that (3) reports the existence in the past (relative to the time of utterance) of a disposition that is sufficient for John's having already reacted with surprise, given the previous fulfilment of a condition itself in the past relative to the time at which the disposition is manifested.[10] What we say is temporally convoluted. A statement like (3) is about the past, relative to the time of utterance, but the specification of what is the case in the past involves some time in the future and also a time that is past relative to that. Why do we feel the need to go in for this degree of convolution?

It seems that this form of words is appropriate when the speaker wishes to indicate that there is now no possibility of the antecedent's being fulfilled. We should see a conditional like:

> 'If Sadie has taken up hang-gliding, she will have taken out adequate life insurance,'

as couched in a form of words which indicates clearly that what is in question is solely what it is legitimate to infer from the information that Sadie has taken up hang-gliding. This use of 'will' is already familiar from sentences not of the conditional form.

---

[9] Notice that, in this case, the 'will' has no sort of future reference.
[10] My analysis diverges considerably from Dudman's at this point.

Hearing the front door bell ring, I may say 'That will be James', where what is in question is what may be inferred from certain information. Where 'will', in this use, occurs in a conditional, what is in question is what could legitimately be inferred from the fulfilment of the condition given in the 'if'-clause.

The effect of reporting this fact about what may be inferred from the fulfilment of the conditional given in the antecedent of the conditional as a fact about the past is to enhance the remoteness of the possibility of the antecedent's being fulfilled. If it is already known that P is not the case, the possibility of learning that P and inferring that Q is no longer a live one. By going in for this degree of temporal convolution in (3), I make suitable acknowledgement of the fact that the fulfilment of the antecedent is not a live possibility.[11]

I have tried to give an account of the logical form of conditionals of the kind that have traditionally been classified as counterfactual, and argued that other conditionals involving 'will' deserve to be included along with them. I have also argued that the materials for an analysis are available in other sentences not of the conditional form, and that these suffice to yield an analysis of traditional counterfactuals.

If the account of 'counterfactual' conditionals that I have sketched is along the right lines, it has a number of wider implications. In the first place, it is misguided to analyse tendencies or dispositions in terms of counterfactuals, since a correct semantic account of them already presupposes that things in the world have them. Secondly, some of the reasons for doubt on whether such conditionals have truth-values turn out to be groundless. There is no reason for denying that they are made true by what is actually the case, but we need to note carefully the temporal location of the states of affairs that make such conditionals true. Finally, the sort of account that I have sketched will explain better than some others that are currently popular some other phenomena associated with 'counterfactual' conditionals.

---

[11] Thus, the Counterfactuality Thesis has this to be said for it: there are certain forms of words that are especially apt in cases where it is known that the question of the fulfilment of the condition specified in the 'if'-clause does not or cannot arise. But, strictly, the falsehood of the antecedent is never actually entailed just by the form of words used, independently of the context.

One such phenomenon is the temporal asymmetry, noted in Section 5, that arises with 'counterfactuals'. This can be explained by the sort of treatment that I am proposing. According to that account, I will assert 'If P had been the case, Q would have been the case' if it was possible to say 'If P is the case, Q will be the case' from an ideal epistemic position before it is settled whether P is the case or not; and that will be so only if matters are so disposed as to ensure the occurrence of Q in the event of P's being the case. In the case of a 'backtracking' conditional, what we should need to have would be a disposition that ensures the *prior* occurrence of Q in the event of P's being the case; but there can be no such disposition, given the direction of causation.

The sort of theory that I have sketched can account for the phenomena that possible-worlds theories have been introduced to accommodate. As we saw in Section 5, questions then arise about how the closeness of possible worlds is to be defined; and it is recognized that, if we are to conform to the judgements about the acceptability of conditionals that we actually make, we need to say that the closest possible world is that which resembles the actual world exactly up to a time in advance of the antecedent's being fulfilled or not, and which matches the actual world exactly in respect of its laws. This is something that is accommodated by the sort of account that I have given, since the ideal epistemic perspective that I suggest is involved in deciding on the acceptability of a forward-looking conditional, and would be one in which we have access to what has occurred up to the relevant time, and also to the general laws and dispositions that are to be found in the actual world. But it avoids the need to import possible worlds into the analysis of these conditionals. 'If P is the case, Q is the case' is made true by what is actually the case now—truths about what has actually occurred, and truths about the way things are disposed to be, in virtue of the laws and other regularities that obtain.

This is reflected in the fact that the approach to 'counterfactuals' that I have sketched is much better equipped than possible-worlds theories to explain conditionals of a different kind from those with which we have so far been concerned. The examples considered so far have had to do with particular events, occurring at particular times, and I have attempted to explain them by appeal to what was available to an ideal perspective at a time *before* the event described in the antecedent has either occurred or not. A 'counterfactual' of the form 'If the square root of two had been rational . . .', with an impossible antecedent, which we saw in Section 5 raises problems for possible-worlds theories, can evidently not be explained in precisely the same way: the antecedent is not about a particular event, which can be considered in advance of its occurrence.

It is, however, possible to see, in outline, how the treatment I have sketched can be extended to apply to such conditionals. Instead of envisaging the epistemic standpoint available before the occurrence, or not, of what is described in the antecedent, someone who considers a hypothesis in ignorance of its truth or falsehood can have other knowledge which can be used to derive consequences from it. But it is also true that someone who *does* know that an antecedent is impossible can adopt the standpoint of someone who lacks such knowledge, and examine what follows in virtue of other knowledge. Here too, 'If P were the case, Q would be the case' is the past tense of 'If P is the case, Q will be the case'. So we can readily assign truth to:

'If there is a largest integer, there is a largest prime number.'

The full working out of the proposal would involve further elaboration of the notion of an ideal epistemic perspective. Such an elaboration would need to attend to our reasons for considering whether to accept or reject a 'counterfactual' conditional. The effect of possible-worlds theories is to suggest that it reflects an interest in engaging in fantasies about how things might have been if certain aspects of the world had been different. Although that interest should not be discounted, if the account of counterfactuals that I have sketched is correct, our interest in knowing whether, if P had been the case, Q would have been, derives from our interest in asking, in advance, whether if P is the case, Q will be. The reason for interest in such questions is evident enough: we need to anticipate future possibilities, and plan for alternative contingencies. It is then understandable that we should later be interested in enquiring whether such a forward-looking conditional was assertible at an earlier time, even though that interest is not a practical one.

# COMMENTARY

# COMMENTARY

## Dorothy Edgington

I have learned much from Michael Woods's splendid essay. In what follows, I try to provide additional background material relevant to his case. Sometimes I add further arguments in support of his conclusions. And sometimes (of course) I register my disagreement with him. I shall say something about each section in turn.

### 1. *Taxonomy*

One current controversy about conditional statements is how to divide the field. In his final section Woods makes an original proposal about the relations between different kinds of conditional. Before we reach that, we need some idea of which conditionals are under discussion at a given stage. Enough of his strategy on taxonomy to meet this need is laid out in Woods's first section.

Traditionally a major distinction has been drawn between 'indicative' conditionals on the one hand, and 'subjunctive' or 'counterfactual' conditionals on the other. The first class has been taken to include:

(1) If he didn't speak to her, he wrote to her;

(2) If he doesn't speak to her, he will write to her;

and the second class:

(3) If he had not spoken to her, he would have written her a letter;

(4) If he were not to speak to her, he would write to her.

Part of the reason the subject took this shape was the prominence of the truth-functional conditional in the logic we inherited from Frege. (1) and (2) are candidates for truth-functional treatment.

Logic textbooks make free use of examples like these. It is, at first sight, plausible that they are equivalent to 'Either he spoke to her or he wrote to her' and 'He will either speak to her or write to her', respectively. And the simplicity and clarity of the truth-functional treatment, and the logic in which it is embedded, makes it worth defending. But no one has seriously maintained that (3) or (4) is truth-functional. Examples of these forms attracted attention among logical empiricists, intent on using Frege's logic to exhibit the structure of scientific discourse. Rudolf Carnap investigated the relation between a dispositional property like being fragile, and its display under suitable conditions: breaking if dropped.[1] The Fregean conditional is unsuitable here: interpreting 'If it is dropped at $t$, it breaks' truth-functionally, it is true provided it is not dropped at $t$. So, it appeared, there is another, non-Fregean conditional construction for us to master: 'If it were the case that . . ., it would be the case that . . .'. It has been a problem ever since.

There is an alternative reaction to the story so far: conditionals are all of a piece, and examples like (3) and (4) make it clear that they are not truth-functional; elementary logic treats of a poor relative of the natural-language 'if'. P. F. Strawson, for instance, gives the examples:

> Remark made in the summer of 1964: 'If Goldwater is elected, then the liberals will be dismayed.'

> Remark made in the winter of 1964: 'If Goldwater had been elected, then the liberals would have been dismayed';

and comments that 'the least attractive thing that one could say about the *difference* between these two remarks is that . . . "if . . . then . . ." has a different meaning in one remark from the meaning which it has in the other'.[2]

However, the existence of pairs of examples like the following:

(5) If Oswald didn't kill Kennedy, someone else did;

---

[1] Rudolf Carnap, 'Testability and Meaning', *Philosophy of Science*, 3 (1936), 419–71; 4 (1937), 1–40.

[2] P. F. Strawson, '"If" and "⊃"', in R. E. Grandy and R. Warner (eds.), *Philosophical Grounds of Rationality* (Oxford, 1986), 230.

(6) If Oswald hadn't killed Kennedy, someone else would have;[3]

seems to support the case for dualism in a theoretically neutral way: whatever the right account of either, they seem to show that there are at least two kinds of conditional. Assume that (5) and (6) each have the form: C(O, S), where C is a conditional operator, O is 'Oswald killed Kennedy', S is 'Someone else killed Kennedy'. Accepting (5) (as we all do) leaves one free to reject (6). So there must be two conditional operators,

> If it is the case that . . ., it is the case that . . .;

> If it were the case that . . ., it would be the case that . . ..

When the sentences which fill the gaps are past tense, the natural way in English to express these two logical forms is by sentences like (5) and (6). Admittedly, the second logical form, with O and S substituted in the gaps, yields something of a monstrosity as an English sentence. But this is a familiar phenomenon in the tradition which began with Frege and Russell: the grammar of natural language often needs substantial revision before it will yield the logical structure of our thoughts. Think of Russell's Theory of Descriptions, of Davidson's 'The Logical Form of Action Sentences',[4] of Frege's innovative treatment of 'All' and 'Some'.

V. H. Dudman, in numerous articles on conditionals from the early 1980s,[5] conducted a vigorous and solitary battle against this cavalier attitude to English grammar. One of his points has struck many philosophers as correct:[6] the line between kinds of conditionals has been misdrawn. Among our initial sample

[3] These examples are due to Ernest Adams, 'Subjunctive and Indicative Conditionals', *Foundations of Language*, 6 (1970), 89–94. As Woods points out, similar examples are found in F. P. Ramsey, 'General Propositions and Causality', in *Foundations of Mathematics* (London, 1931).

[4] Donald Davidson, 'The Logical Form of Action Sentences', in *Essays on Actions and Events* (Oxford, 1980), 105–48.

[5] See, for instance, 'Tense and Time in English Verb Clusters of the Primary Pattern', *Australian Journal of Linguistics*, 3 (1983), 25–44; 'Parsing "If"-Sentences', *Analysis*, 44 (1984), 145–53; 'Indicative and Subjunctive', *Analysis*, 48 (1988), 113–22; 'Vive la Revolution!', *Mind*, 98 (1989), 591–603.

[6] See, for instance, Timothy Smiley, 'Hunter on Conditionals', *Proceedings of the Aristotelian Society*, 84 (1983–4), 241–9; Bennett, 'Farewell to the Phlogiston Theory of Conditionals'; D. H. Mellor, 'How to Believe a Conditional', *Journal of Philosophy*, 90, No. 5 (1993), 233–48.

sentences, (1) is the odd man out. Sentences (2), (3), and (4)—the 'wills' and 'woulds'—belong together, he argues: they differ only in tense, not in embodying different species of conditional. Return to Strawson's pair of examples about Goldwater. Strawson's comment (Dudman will agree) is immensely plausible. Again, suppose I change my travel plans on being told, 'If you travel on Friday, it will cost £20 extra.' I discover I was misinformed—if I had travelled on Friday, it would not have cost me extra. The same thought is expressed, in different contexts, first with a 'will', then with a 'would'.

Dudman discerns a grammatical feature which (2)–(4) have in common, differentiating them from (1). In (1) we easily identify two contained sentences. In (2)–(4), the verb in the 'if'-clause has a tense which seems to be inappropriate for its apparent meaning in the conditional. Consider:

(7) If it rains tomorrow, they will cancel the trip;

(8) If it had rained today, they would have cancelled the trip;

(9) If it rained tomorrow, they would cancel the trip.

'It rains tomorrow' is not a sentence—except possibly as a statement of intention on the part of the Almighty, but that is irrelevant to its use in (7). Similarly for (8) and (9): in each we have a *backwards tense shift* in the 'if'-clause. However this is to be explained, it provides some reason for expecting a uniform explanation of (2)–(4), and of (7)–(9).

It emerges in the final section of his essay that Woods follows Dudman in placing 'wills' with 'woulds': 'My dogmatic slumbers on the subject of so-called counterfactual conditionals, though not first disturbed, were fully dispelled by the work of Vic Dudman' (p. 78). The ground is prepared in Woods's opening section, first by his arguing that neither 'subjunctive' nor 'counterfactual' is a helpful label. 'The subjunctive exists only vestigially in English' (p. 5). No one has much of an explanation of why some conditionals should require this vestige, and others forbid it. No one has linked these conditionals to other vestiges of the subjunctive. Nowhere else in philosophy does 'subjunctive' do any theoretical work. (Woods does allow that e.g. 'If he were here now, he would be surprised' is in the subjunctive mood. But only inelegance mitigates against replacing 'were' by 'was'.)

'Counterfactual' is no better. No one uses it to mean 'conditional with a false antecedent': half of all conditionals have false antecedents. No one insists that for a counterfactual statement to be true or correct, the antecedent must be false. Many claim that for a conditional of this form to be appropriately used, the speaker must take the antecedent to be false. Even if this were so, it would be mysterious that this pragmatic feature should require a distinct kind of conditional on which to operate. And Woods shows that it is not so: 'there is no class of conditionals that convey that the speaker believes the antecedent to be false in virtue of their verbal form alone' (p. 6). John denied that he took the money. 'But if he had taken the money, he would have denied it,' you say. Far from suggesting that you think he didn't take the money, you convey that you are unimpressed with his denial as affording a reason to think he didn't.

Woods has helped me to see the importance of this blatantly non-counterfactual use of 'counterfactuals'—which, perhaps because of the label, has been largely ignored. The doctor examines the patient and discovers certain symptoms. 'If he had taken arsenic, he would have just these symptoms,' she says.[7] 'A bus is coming.' 'How do you know?' (for the traffic is concealed from view). 'People at the bus stop are shuffling forward—that's what they would be doing if a bus were coming.' You use the 'counterfactual' in giving your reason for thinking the antecedent to be true. 'I infer that the prisoner jumped from this window; for the flowers below have been damaged—and they would have been damaged if he had jumped from the window.' Note that the conditionals in such reasoning are essentially 'woulds': I can see that the flowers have been damaged—they have been damaged, whether or not he jumped. The questions are whether they *would have been* damaged if he had jumped, and would not have been damaged if he had not. This mode of thinking is fundamental to empirical reasoning—which hypothesis H is such that what we do observe is what we *would* observe if H were true? The same 'would'-conditional may be used in one context to argue for the truth of its antecedent, in another to argue for the falsity of its antecedent. 'If that bird were a canary, it would be yellow.' Said of a visibly blue bird, I argue that it is not a canary. Said of a

[7] See Anderson, 'A Note on Subjunctive and Counterfactual Conditionals'.

visibly yellow bird, I present a reason for thinking I was right when I said it was a canary.

Like Dudman, Woods distinguishes the class of conditionals constructed in a straightforward manner out of two simpler sentences, those like (1) and (5), from the rest. Woods calls these 'Simple Conditionals'. But unlike Dudman,[8] he is disinclined to the view that 'if' performs a different role in Simple Conditionals from the rest:

> we should not regard 'counterfactual' conditional sentences as simply resulting from the application of 'If . . . then . . .' to a pair of sentences. The distinctive syntactic features of 'counterfactual' conditional sentences are found elsewhere; most obviously in the past tense (even if that tense does not work in the same way inside an 'if'-clause as it does elsewhere), but also in expressions like 'would' and 'would have'. Compare 'I thought she would come' and 'In 1932, he would have been under twelve years old'. So it is natural to look for an explanation of the meaning of 'counterfactual' conditionals given in terms of the general meaning of 'If . . . then . . .', as found in Simple Conditionals, and the semantic properties of the past tense and of 'would', etc., as found elsewhere. (p. 10)

This is a noble aim. Received philosophical theories aside, there is not much of a case for thinking that 'if' is ambiguous. There is, admittedly, the Oswald–Kennedy phenomenon. But Woods's aim is to understand the difference between (5) and (6) in terms of a single 'if', different tenses, and the effect of 'would'. Simple Conditionals are to be studied first, then, not only for their own sake, but because they contribute to the meaning of the others. And conditionals with 'will' appearing in the consequent, like (2) and (7), are *sub judice* until Woods's final section.

This has the effect of restricting Woods's choice of examples in the bulk of the essay: no 'If it rains tomorrow . . .' or 'If you strike the match . . .' examples are allowed. One place where this is slightly awkward for him is in his brief discussion of conditional commands (Section 7, p. 75), which he construes as 'If P, then do X'. The most common conditional commands are of the form 'If it rains this afternoon, stay indoors'—that is, their antecedents are like those of 'will'-conditionals, not those of

---

[8] Dudman gives a quite different account of Simple Conditionals (which he calls 'hypotheticals') and the others. See his 'Parsing "If"-Sentences'.

Simple Conditionals. And Woods's only example of a conditional command, 'If John calls [this afternoon], tell him that I have gone out' (ibid.), seems to be an infringement of his practice of avoiding this sort of antecedent. Admittedly, 'John calls this afternoon' can be used as a self-standing sentence, to express the thought that this has already been fixed. But that usage is as irrelevant to its use as an antecedent as a remark of the Almighty, 'It rains tomorrow,' is to the use of that sentence as an antecedent. When I discuss Woods's final section, I will return to the case for segregating 'will'-conditionals from Simple Conditionals.

## 2. *Assertibility*

In the next six sections the case for and against the various candidate accounts of Simple Conditionals is assessed. In Section 2 we are introduced to the suspects: the truth-functional account (together with some way of defusing its apparently paradoxical consequences); the idea that an 'if'-statement is used to make a conditional assertion of the consequent; the claim that Simple Conditionals have stronger-than-truth-functional truth-conditions; the view that they are not candidates for evaluation in terms of truth. Woods rejects the view that the truth of 'If P then Q' requires some 'connection' between antecedent and consequent: if I'm sure it was a good party, but don't know whether John was there, I'm sure it was a good party whether or not John was there, and hence that it was a good party if John was there, and a good party if he was not (though it would generally be misleading for me to assert these conditionals). And he points out that where there is a connection, it may be only epistemic—a connection amongst the speaker's beliefs. 'If he didn't tell John to bring the hammer, he told Fred,' I say, for I heard the foreman tell someone to do so, and only John and Fred were around. There is a discussion of Ramsey's famous footnote about 'adding P hypothetically to your stock of knowledge, and arguing on that basis about Q', which is more fully developed in the next section.

'Assertibility-conditions' are introduced in this section as an important theoretical tool—first as a possible means of defusing objections to the truth-functional conditional: 'One thing that commands general agreement is that the *assertibility-conditions* of natural language conditionals do not coincide with the *truth-conditions* of the corresponding material conditionals' (p. 12).

But independently of this setting, Woods accords this notion a central role: 'it must be one of the tasks of the theorist of conditionals to state clearly in what their assertibility-conditions consist' (p. 13), and reference to assertibility recurs throughout his essay.

A warning is called for, I think: this is a dangerously slippery notion. So many, and so diverse, are the factors relevant to whether you should (may, would) assert a given proposition on a given occasion, that any theoretical deployment of the notion must be somewhat abstract, and focus on some aspects of what makes a proposition assertible. Different theorists focus on different aspects, for different purposes. There are at least four nonequivalent ways in which the term has been used.

(1) In Michael Dummett's work, the question of the 'assertibility' of a proposition is a question of the speaker's having adequate evidence or grounds for it.[9] (A proposition may be true but unassertible by a speaker; and conversely, when evidence is defeasible, a proposition may be assertible but false.)

(2) In some writings on conditionals it is assumed as a general principle that a proposition is assertible by a subject if and only if he assigns it a high subjective probability—roughly, a proposition is assertible if and only if it is believed.[10] This is potentially different from (1): something may be believed unjustifiably, and someone may have adequate grounds for a proposition yet not believe it. Even if (1) and (2) coincide in normal cases, their focus is different. (2) is silent about grounds or evidence for beliefs or assertions.

(3) H. P. Grice pointed out that a proposition may be accepted as true on adequate grounds, while it is nevertheless *not* assertible without seriously misleading one's audience: to assert it would violate principles governing conversation.[11] In particular,

---

[9] See, for example, the Preface to Dummett, *Truth and Other Enigmas.*

[10] David Lewis, 'Probabilities of Conditionals and Conditional Probabilities', *Philosophical Papers*, ii. 133: 'Assertibility goes by subjective probability.' See also Anthony Appiah, *Assertion and Conditionals* (Cambridge, 1985), and Frank Jackson, *Conditionals.* (NB: opinion is divided between 'assertibility' and 'assertability'. Jackson marks a distinction between two uses of the notion by the two spellings. Here I follow Woods and stick to the middle-letter-i spelling.)

[11] Grice, William James Lectures, in *Studies in the Way of Words.*

one should not say something weaker than some other relevant thing one is in a position to say. 'You won't eat those and live,' I say of some wholesome and delicious mushrooms—knowing that you will now leave them alone, deferring to my expertise. I say nothing false—for indeed you don't eat them—but of course I mislead you.[12] The Gricean notion and the Dummettian one can pull in opposite directions. For Dummett, a canonical ground for the assertibility of a disjunction is the verification of one disjunct. For Grice, this is a case when asserting the disjunction would violate conversational maxims: in general, one should assert a disjunction only if one has not verified either disjunct.

(4) Jackson claims that it is part of the meaning of certain words like 'but', 'however', 'even', and 'if', that they endow utterances in which they occur with special 'assertibility-conditions'.[13] The truth-conditions of 'A but B' are those of 'A and B'; but to understand 'but' is to know when it is correct to assert the former rather than the latter.

Each of these uses of 'assertibility' gives rise to further complications. For (1) and (2), there is the highly context-dependent matter of how good my grounds have to be, or how close to certain I must be, to justify an assertion unqualified by 'Probably', or 'I think'. Nor is it merely a question of how strong the evidence, how close to certain, but perhaps also, of the nature and prominence of the risk of error. Some have the intuition that one should not assert, unqualified, 'He will not win the lottery,' even if the chance of error is only, say, one in twenty million; whereas we would readily assert 'Spurs beat Liverpool,' having consulted the newspaper, even if results are misreported considerably more often than once in twenty million times. Further along Grice's path, there are innumerable considerations of ethics, etiquette, or prudence which would make it outrageous to voice certain opinions to certain audiences.

Woods convinces me that the phenomena to which Jackson assimilates 'if' should not be treated in terms of 'assertibility-conditions' at all. 'But' is Jackson's favourite example. Grant that 'A and B' and 'A but B' have the same truth-conditions, yet differ

---

[12] See Lewis, 'Probabilities of Conditionals and Conditional Probabilities', *Philosophical Papers*, ii. 143.

[13] Jackson, *Conditionals*, ch. 2.

in meaning: it is a semantic property of the latter that it is used to signal a contrast between the two propositions. This contrast, however, can be signalled whether or not 'A but B' is *asserted*, Woods points out (p. 61): 'If she was born in Turin but left when she was three, she doesn't know Italy well.' 'Either he arrived on time but gave up waiting for us, or he never arrived at all.' Further, 'but' also occurs in commands and questions: 'Shut the window but leave the door open'; 'Does anyone want eggs but no ham?' Assertibility-conditions do not mark the essence of the difference between 'and' and 'but'. Similar points could be made about 'even', 'however', and so on.

Considering the objection that it would be better to focus on acceptability than assertibility, Woods demurs because 'the phenomena that a theory of conditionals is directly answerable to are those of actual use. Presumably, the assertibility-conditions of conditionals will, in their turn, determine the conditions in which they are accepted' (p. 13).

But, given the factors extraneous to semantics which affect whether someone will say something in given circumstances, it is easy to misread these data of actual use, or their armchair surrogate, 'Would you *say* so-and-so, in such-and-such circumstances?' It was Grice's salutary lesson that having adequate reasons for taking something to be true (i.e. for accepting it), and having adequate reasons for asserting it, can come spectacularly apart. Following some philosophers of language (Quine, Davidson), the 'field linguist' does better to prompt assent to and dissent from sentences, rather than merely to observe what people say. Grice predicts that there are sentences to which you will assent, in a context in which it is understood that the questioner merely wants to elicit your opinions (which you have no motive to hide), whereas you would not assert these sentences spontaneously. Grice is no doubt correct. But this distinction of Grice's does not vindicate his diagnosis of the truth-conditions of conditionals: we dissent from conditionals which we would have every reason to take as true if they were interpreted truth-functionally.

Although little harm is done, Woods's liking for assertibility-conditions leads him to expound positions in these terms when this was not the intention of their authors. The so-called 'Ramsey Test' is primarily an account of degree of conditional belief, not assertion. Ernest Adams did speak of 'assertibility' in his earliest writings on conditionals, but by the time he wrote *The Logic of Conditionals*, he had abandoned this notion as potentially misleading.

In some contexts in which Woods uses the notion, it is unclear which reading of it is at stake. For instance, he makes the following criticism of Grice (p. 36): while Grice can explain why we don't assert 'If A, B' on the sole grounds that ¬A, he cannot explain why we sometimes do, and sometimes do not, assert 'If A, B' on the sole grounds that B. The kind of case Woods has in mind is this. I believe that the match has been cancelled, because all the players went down with 'flu. So I accept that the match has been cancelled, whether or not rain was forecast: I accept that if rain was forecast, the match has been cancelled, and if rain was not forecast, the match has been cancelled. But I don't accept that if the players made a very speedy recovery, the match was cancelled.

The phenomena to be explained are real on the reading of 'assertible' which stays in line with 'acceptable'. But in the sense of 'assertible' with which Grice's work is concerned, I would not assert, in this situation, 'If rain was forecast, the match has been cancelled'; for I would be making a misleadingly weak claim. There only appears to be a difficulty for Grice if we run together different notions of assertibility.

## 3. *Ramsey and Adams*

Section 3 discusses the idea, found in Ramsey's footnote of 1929, and developed by Ernest Adams, that one's degree of confidence that if A, B should be understood in terms of the concept: the conditional probability of B given A. This concept is, unfortunately, not a standard tool of the philosopher's trade. Clear and accurate as Woods's exposition is, I shall nevertheless try further to explain and motivate Ramsey's idea.

We are often not sure whether if P, Q: we make uncertain judgements of this kind. I may think it likely, but less than certain, that if John caught the eight o'clock train, he is in his office now. If the truth-conditions of conditionals were unproblematic, uncertain judgements would create no special problem: they would be judgements of uncertainty about the fulfilment of the truth-conditions. Contraposing, it is a test of the adequacy of proposed truth-conditions that they have plausible consequences for uncertain conditional judgements. (It is unduly narrow, in assessing proposed truth-conditions, to restrict one's thought-experiments to the special cases of *certain* acceptance and rejection.) The truth-functional account scores badly on this test. Suppose I think it unlikely that John caught the eight o'clock train (more likely, he did not catch it), and also think it unlikely that if he did catch the train, he is now in the office. On the truth-functional account of the conditional, these are inconsistent opinions, for to think it likely that the antecedent is false is to think it likely that a sufficient condition for the truth of the conditional is satisfied. As my opinions appear manifestly consistent, this counts against the truth-functional proposal.

Consider the proposal that some stronger condition is required for the truth of the conditional, for instance, that the consequent be deducible from the antecedent together with other suitable facts, so that, given the circumstances, the antecedent *guarantees* the truth of the consequent. Now I can think it likely that if John caught the train, he is now in the office, while denying that circumstances are such that the truth of the antecedent guarantees the consequent. Trains, and John, are not that predictable. I can be sure that this truth-condition is *not* satisfied, while my experience of trains and John's habits makes me, say, 95 per cent certain that if he caught the train, he is now in the office. The case of the uncertain conditional judgement counts also against this strong truth-condition: if it were correct, I should have no confidence at all that if John caught the train he is now in the office.

The same point may be made with an artificial numerical example: how confident should you be that if the die lands an even number, it will land a six? Well, there are three ways of landing even, and one of them is six: the natural answer is $\frac{1}{3}$. On the truth-functional account of the matter, the answer is $\frac{2}{3}$: four out of the six ways the die can land (1, 3, 5, 6) make the truth-functional conditional true. On the requirement of a strong connection, the answer is zero: you have no confidence at all that the antecedent guarantees the truth of the consequent.

Let us put truth-conditions aside for the remainder of this section, and focus on the nature of uncertain conditional judgements. Ramsey put it thus in 1929:

If two people are arguing 'If P, will Q?' and are both in doubt as to P, they are adding P hypothetically to their stock of knowledge and arguing on that basis about Q; . . . they are fixing their degrees of belief in Q given P.[14]

You arrive at a conditional judgement by *supposing* that the antecedent is true; and making a judgement about the consequent *under that supposition*.

'Degree of belief in Q given P' comes from Ramsey's earlier paper in which he argued that probability theory provides a 'logic of partial belief'. Your degree of closeness to certainty that P he called your 'degree of belief in P', and your degree of closeness to certainty that Q, on the supposition that P, he called your 'degree of belief in Q given P'. Making the idealizing assumption that these can be represented by numbers between 1 and 0, he stated as a 'fundamental law of probable belief':

Degree of belief in (P and Q) = degree of belief in P × degree of belief in Q given P.[15]

This is a deployment of a standard principle of probability theory. Thomas Bayes wrote in 1763:

The probability that two events . . . will both happen is . . . the probability of the first [multiplied by] the probability of the second *on the supposition that the first happens*. (My emphasis)

The concept of conditional probability has been around for some time. It is needed to calculate the probability of a conjunction. Let us try to understand why the above principle holds. On the following page is a Venn Diagram. This represents a space of possibilities whose finest division is into four exclusive and jointly exhaustive parts: A & B, A & ¬B, ¬A & B, ¬A & ¬B. A probability distribution over these possibilities assigns a non-negative number to each of the four parts in such a way that the numbers

---

[14] 'General Propositions and Causality', 247.
[15] 'Truth and Probability', 181.

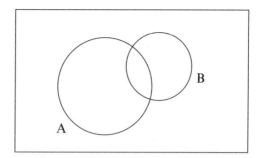

sum to 1 (the number assigned to a certainty).[16] Equivalently, let the area of the whole rectangle be 1, and let the areas of the four parts represent their probabilities. For example, if ¼ of the whole area is (A & ¬B), this represents Prob(A & ¬B) = ¼. Note that the area which represents A splits into two parts, A & B, A & ¬B; so any probability distribution is such that Prob(A) = Prob(A & B) + Prob(A & ¬B).

The conditional probability of B given A may be explained thus, with reference to the diagram. Suppose that A; that is, hypothetically eliminate all the ¬A-possibilities, so that only the A-circle remains. Under that supposition, how likely is it that B? That is, how likely is it that B, in the sub-space of possibilities in which A is true? In terms of the Venn Diagram, the question is: what proportion *of the A-part* is a B-part? The A-part splits into the A & B-part and the A & ¬B-part. The answer is given by

(CP) Prob(B given A) = $\dfrac{\text{Prob(A \& B)}}{\text{Prob(A)}}$.

This is equivalent to Ramsey's and Bayes's principle above.

If Prob(A) = ½ and Prob(A & B) and Prob(A & ¬B) are each ¼, then Prob(B given A) = ½: ½ of the A-part is a B-part. If Prob(A & ¬B) = 0, all of the A-part is A & B, so the ratio is 1; if Prob(A & B) = 0, the ratio is 0. (These last are the special cases of acceptance and rejection with certainty.) Note that the thought experiment requires that Prob(A) ≠ 0. If Prob(A) = 0, Prob(B given A) does not exist.

---

[16] More generally, a probability distribution is an assignment of non-negative numbers to each of a set of exclusive and exhaustive possibilities, in such a way that the numbers sum to 1.

It is important to note the following, which is what makes the concept important: we can assign a value to Prob(B given A) without knowing Prob(A) or Prob(A & B). Here is a simple example. You are to pick a card at random from a well-shuffled pile which you know to contain three kings, one red and two black. The probability that you will pick a black card, given that you pick a king, is then ⅔. You don't need to be told how likely it is that you will pick a king, nor how likely it is that you will pick a black king (that is, you don't need to be told how many cards there are in the pile) to know that it is ⅔ as likely that you will pick a black king, as it is that you will pick a king. (CP) should not be construed as a reductive definition of conditional probability in terms of unconditional probability, then, as though the left-hand side were merely short for the right. It does appear as such in formal, abstract, axiomatic theories of probability, which are under no obligation to respect conceptual priorities. Such theories are relatively recent. If the concept had been introduced as a mere abbreviation for the ratio on the right, it would be of little use. Instead, the concept was introduced as a route to the probability of a conjunction.

To see why the notion is needed, consider first this special case. Suppose the propositions A and B are independent: whether one is true has nothing whatsoever to do with whether the other is true, and this is known. Suppose the probability of A is ½ and the probability of B is ¼. What then can we say about the probability of (A & B)?

Here I choose a different representation of the problem (see the diagram on p. 110). We first divide our space of possibilities into A and ¬A, each with probability ½. We then subdivide each part further: split A into (A & B) and (A & ¬B), and similarly ¬A into (¬A & B) and (¬A & ¬B). As A and B are independent, the probability of B (¼) is not affected by whether A. So A's probability of ½ splits into Prob(A & B): ¼ of ½ = ⅛; Prob(A & ¬B): ¾ of ½ = ⅜. So we have

If A and B are independent, Prob(A & B) = Prob(A) × Prob(B).

Although the notion of conditional probability does not appear in the above formula, it was appealed to in its justification: when A and B are independent, the probability of B on the assumption

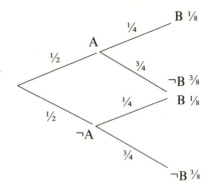

that A is the same as the probability of B on the assumption that ¬A, and is the same as the probability of B. Now consider the probability of a conjunction when we drop the assumption of independence: assuming that A is true makes some difference to how likely it is that B is true. For example, I am wondering how likely it is that John will pass the test. The examiner is to choose at random one of two topics, A and another. On the assumption that A is chosen, it's around 90 per cent likely that he will pass. On the assumption that A is not chosen, it's only around 50 per cent likely that he will pass.

Here, 90 per cent of the 50 per cent probability of topic A, goes to (topic A and pass). Fifty per cent of the 50 per cent probability of ¬A is the probability of (¬A and pass). The probability that he will pass is the sum of the probabilities of (A and pass) and (¬A and pass), which is (90 per cent of 50 per cent) + (50 per cent of 50 per cent) = 70 per cent or 0.7.

We have estimated the probability that he will pass (B) by the following route:

Prob(B) = Prob(A & B) + Prob(¬A & B)
       = Prob(A)Prob(B given A) + Prob(¬A)Prob(B given ¬A).

This is one illustration of our use of the concept of conditional probability in the calculation of an unconditional probability.

Ramsey's suggestion, then, was that assessing a conditional, you suppose that the antecedent is true, and assess the consequent under that hypothesis; and this has the structure of a

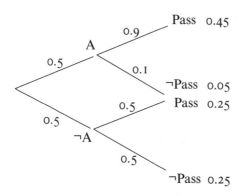

judgement of conditional probability. This idea lay dormant until the 1960s, when several philosophers sought illumination about conditionals from this source. In particular, Ernest Adams developed a logic for a language with conditionals construed in accordance with (CP). Adams discovered an important property of classically valid arguments—that they are, in a special, precise sense, probability-preserving. Call the uncertainty of a proposition one minus its probability. Then, if an argument is necessarily truth-preserving, it has the following property: there is no probability function over its sentences such that the uncertainty of the conclusion exceeds the sum of the uncertainties of its premisses. This vindicates our accepting a proposition which we deduce from two or three premisses of which we are nearly but not quite certain: our high degree of confidence in the premisses does place an upper limit on the uncertainty of our conclusion. Now Adams applied this idea to arguments involving conditionals: call the uncertainty of 'If A, B' one minus the conditional probability of B given A. Call an argument valid if there is no probability function in which the uncertainty of the conclusion exceeds the sum of the uncertainties of the premisses. And a logic for conditionals emerges which is now well known. (It is the same as Stalnaker's logic, and Lewis's for counterfactuals, when these are restricted to sentences which do not contain embedded conditionals.)

While generally sympathetic to this approach, Woods ends this section with some difficulties. The first is that 'the conditional probability of B given A' only exists when the probability of A is not zero. But we do, he says, use Simple Conditionals when we are sure that the antecedent is false, for instance, when we argue by *reductio*: 'If the square root of 2 is rational, then . . ..'

Now, there may be other problems about the treatment of logical and mathematical conditionals in this framework, independent of antecedents with zero probability, but I put them aside.

The restriction to antecedents with non-zero probability is supposed to fit the thesis that, when a Simple Conditional is used, the antecedent is taken as an epistemic possibility, as not certainly false, by the thinker (speaker). Certainty is a vague and shifty notion—there is no sharp context-free distinction between it and its near neighbours. There are few things that you *cannot* take as an epistemic possibility, as not certainly false, even if you standardly do not—as all the famous sceptical hypotheses show. Descartes searched for such things, and his findings lend some support to this restriction on Simple Conditionals: is there any thought to be had which begins 'If I don't exist now . . .'?

With Woods's example one can say two things. First, nothing is lost by construing the conditional 'If the square root of 2 *were* rational, then . . .', i.e. as 'subjunctive' or 'counterfactual'. Then, whatever the difficulties in understanding it, the problem is not one of certainty that the antecedent is false, which is often the case with such forms. Second, if you are already sure that the antecedent is false, you are not performing the *reductio* for your own benefit, but for that of an audience: *you* are not supposing the antecedent to be true, you are asking your audience to do so, to see what follows. You pretend to adopt their point of view—of not knowing, until they are shown, that the square root of 2 is irrational. If you were seriously to take on board the supposition that it is rational, you would say something like 'If the square root of 2 is rational, then there must be something wrong with that proof!' Compare 'If Elizabeth I didn't die in 1603, the history books are wrong'; as opposed to 'If she hadn't died in 1603, then . . .'; though, adopting the perspective of your less well-informed audience, you might say 'If she didn't die in 1603, James I didn't ascend the throne at the age of . . .'.

Woods's second difficulty is a little puzzling. It is described as a case in which 'someone is ready to assert a conditional, but, on learning that the antecedent is true, declines to infer that the consequent is true' (p. 29). But Woods has already recognized such cases: at the end of Section 2 he mentions an example of Jackson's, 'If Reagan is bald, no one outside his immediate family knows it.' I may believe the consequent on the *hypothesis* that the antecedent is true. But if I learn that the antecedent is true, I abandon the conditional rather than infer the consequent. Ramsey, too, was aware of such cases: he warned against misinterpreting 'your degree of belief in B given A' as the degree of belief you would have in B if you learned A.[17] The 'test' for belief in a conditional—would I believe B if I learned A?—should not be associated with Ramsey's name.

In Woods's example, you start off accepting 'If John is not at home, he is in his office'. You then discover that he is not in his office. Woods says you still accept 'If he is not at home, he is in his office'. Then you discover that he is not at home, and abandon the conditional rather than infer the consequent.

It is not a problem for Ramsey or Adams that you abandon the conditional rather than infer the consequent, as we have seen. But they cannot agree with Woods that you may still accept 'If he is not at home, he is in his office' when you discover for certain that he is not in his office. If you take it as an epistemic possibility that he is not at home, you are still sure, on this assumption, that he is *not* in his office. And if you do not take it as an epistemic possibility that he is not at home, we have the zero-antecedent problem—the conditional probability doesn't exist. Ramsey and Adams would insist that, on learning that he is not in the office, your earlier conditional thought needs rephrasing: if he were not at home, he would be in the office. (Looking ahead to Woods's final section: this expresses the belief that the relevant conditional probability (in office given not at home) *was* high; although it is no longer high, now that you know he is not in the office.) This, too, will be abandoned if you learn that he is not at home. But that is no special problem.

## 4. *Truth-Values*

If one is impressed by Ramsey's account of conditional degree of belief, and the logic which Adams constructed for it, a natural

---

[17] Ramsey, 'Truth and Probability', in *Foundations of Mathematics*, 180.

question to ask is: what truth-conditions can we assign to a conditional which fit this account of conditional belief? Which proposition has truth-conditions such that one's degree of belief in its truth must match one's degree of belief in B given A? Robert Stalnaker asked that question, and thought he had answered it, until David Lewis showed that there are no such truth-conditions, no proposition at all such that your degree of belief in its truth systematically matches your degree of belief in B given A.[18]

The word 'systematically' matters. In a given belief state, there may of course be a proposition C (or several such propositions) such that, *per accidens*, Prob(C) = Prob(B given A). But if someone else, or you in a different belief state, might consistently have Prob(C) ≠ Prob(B given A), C is not the required proposition. The question was whether there is a proposition C such that in *any* consistent belief state in which the relevant propositions figure, and Prob(A) ≠ 0, Prob(C) = Prob(B given A), i.e. Prob(A & B)/Prob(A).

Woods indicated his intention to provide details of Lewis's famous result. I shall not give Lewis's proof.[19] It is a completely cogent proof of an important conclusion, a remarkable discovery of his. But, in my view, it gives little explanatory insight as to *why* the result holds: why there is no proposition the probability of whose truth systematically matches the conditional probability of B given A. In my view, the two arguments I shall give do rather better on that score.

Let A and B be any two logically independent propositions. Suppose for *reductio* that there is a proposition C such that, for all probability assignments to the relevant propositions which assign a non-zero probability to A,

---

[18] See Stalnaker, 'A Theory of Conditionals' and 'Indicative Conditionals'; Lewis, 'Probabilities of Conditionals and Conditional Probabilities'.

[19] I give a version of Lewis's proof, from weaker assumptions than his, in 'On Conditionals', *Mind*, 104 (1995), §6.3, 275–6, and a more faithful reproduction of the original in 'The Mystery of the Missing Matter of Fact', *Proceedings of the Aristotelian Society Supplementary Volume*, 65 (1991),197. Lewis's original paper, 'Probabilities of Conditionals and Conditional Probabilities', is reprinted in Harper, Stalnaker, and Pearce (eds.), *Ifs*, 129–47, in Lewis, *Philosophical Papers*, ii. 133–52, and in Jackson (ed.), *Conditionals*, 76–101. Lewis gave further proofs, from weaker assumptions, in his 'Probabilities of Conditionals and Conditional Probabilities II', *Philosophical Review*, 5 (1986), 581–9, also reprinted in Jackson (ed.), *Conditionals*, 102–10.

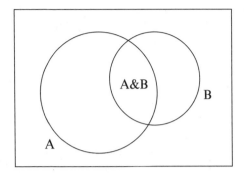

$$\text{Prob}(C) = \frac{\text{Prob}(A \& B)}{\text{Prob}(A)}$$

(call this 'the Equation').

Above, again, is a Venn diagram. The proportion of the rectangle which is A represents the probability of A. The conditional probability of B given A is represented by the proportion *of A* which is B. Note that (i) the conditional probability of B given A depends only upon how we distribute probabilities *in the part of the space in which A is true*. What happens in the ¬A-part of the space has no bearing on it. But (ii) any proposition C which has any hope of being the conditional proposition we seek must be true in some but not all ¬A-possibilities. (If this were not so, C would be a proposition entailed by ¬A; or one which entails A. It is easy to exclude such cases, by showing that there are probability distributions in which their probability would not equal Prob(B given A).)[20] But (iii) there are distinct probability distributions which agree in the A-part, hence agree on Prob(B given A), yet disagree in the ¬A-part, hence disagree on Prob(¬A & C). As Prob(C) = Prob(A & C) + Prob(¬A & C), they disagree on Prob(C). Return to the Venn diagram. Imagine everything in the A-circle to be fixed. Now divide the ¬A-part in two any way you like. Call the two parts '¬A & C' and '¬A & ¬C'. Different divi-

---

[20] (a) Suppose ¬A entailed C. Then we could not have Prob(¬A) high and Prob(C) low. But we can have Prob(¬A) high and Prob(B given A) low. So Prob(C) would not equal Prob(B given A) in all distributions. (b) Suppose C entailed A. Then we could not have Prob(C) high and Prob(A) low. But we can have Prob(B given A) high and Prob(A) low. So Prob(C) would not equal Prob(B given A) in all distributions.

sions determine different probabilities for C (which are got by adding a fixed Prob(A & C) to a variable Prob(¬A & C). But they have no effect on Prob(B given A), which is unaltered by any change in the ¬A-probabilities.

This is the mathematical fact: take any two logically independent propositions A and B. There is no proposition C such that in all probability distributions over the relevant propositions, Prob(C) = Prob(B given A) (i.e. Prob(A & B)/Prob(A)). I now try to show how this mathematical fact illuminates the philosophical issue. We show that the interpretation of conditional degree of belief as conditional probability (call this interpretation CB) has two virtues—two nice features. The truth-functional conditional has the first but not the second. Any stronger, non-truth-functional conditional has the second but not the first. Indeed, no proposition has both. And this fact can be explained in terms of the mathematical fact just mentioned. The two features are these:

(1) Minimal certainty that ¬(A & ¬B) (ruling out just A & ¬B) is enough for certainty that if A, B. (Minimal certainty that A ∨ B (ruling out just ¬A & ¬B) is sufficient for certainty that if ¬A, B; minimal certainty that ¬(A & B) (ruling out just A & B) is enough for certainty that if A, ¬B).

(2) It is not necessarily irrational to have a high degree of belief in ¬A yet a low degree of belief that if A, B.

The truth-functional account satisfies (1) but not (2): A ⊃ B is true if ¬A, so a high degree of belief that ¬A is inconsistent with a low degree of belief that A ⊃ B. Stronger, non-truth-functional truth-conditions may satisfy (2), but cannot satisfy (1): for any stronger truth-condition, ruling out A & ¬B leaves open the possibility that 'If A, B' is false. (CB) satisfies both (1) and (2): ruling out just A & ¬B makes Prob(B given A) = 1; and it is possible to have Prob(¬A) high yet Prob(B given A) low.

Take any proposition. Substitute it for 'If A, B' in (1) and (2). Now either this proposition is entailed by A ⊃ B, or it is not. If it is, it will satisfy (1) but not (2). If it is not, it may satisfy (2), but cannot satisfy (1). (CB) satisfies both (1) and (2). So it cannot be equivalent to a degree of belief in any proposition.

How does CB achieve what the probability of no proposition can? Well, (1) certainty that A & ¬B is false (in the absence of certainty that A is false) is enough for certainty that B given A, *not* because some proposition A*B is held to be true whenever A & ¬B is false, but because B is held to be true in all the 'worlds'[21] that concern the question whether, if A, B—*the A-worlds*. What goes on in the ¬A-worlds has nothing to do with how likely it is that B is true if A is. (2) A high degree of belief that ¬A is consistent with a low degree of belief that B if A, *not* because some proposition A*B may be false in some ¬A-worlds, but because the fact that Prob(¬A) is high has no bearing at all on whether most, or the most probable, A-worlds are B-worlds.

Pre-theoretically, we can discern a difference between believing that B *on the supposition that A*; and believing that something is true, *simpliciter*; between asserting that B *on the condition that A*; and asserting something, *simpliciter*. Yet it was not obvious that the first could not be reduced to the second: that there is nothing that I believe *simpliciter* if and only if I believe that B on the supposition that A, and assert *simpliciter* if and only if I assert that B on the condition that A. The above arguments show that these two kinds of mental state and speech act are irreducibly distinct.

It is wrong to think of this as a probabilistic account of conditionals. It is a probabilistic account of degree of belief, in which we find at hand an account of degree of conditional belief. There are conditional desires, hopes, fears, etc., as well as conditional beliefs. There are conditional commands, questions, etc., as well as conditional statements. Any propositional attitude can occur *simpliciter*, or under a supposition. Any speech act can be performed unconditionally or conditionally. It just so happens that the first theoretical use of conditionality seems to have occurred in probability theory.

Woods says (p. 32) that one may still keep the Equation and construe 'If A, B' as expressing a proposition, provided that *the proposition it expresses is relative to a belief state*. As far as Lewis's proof and my arguments go, this is so. But there are now so many proofs: Stalnaker (having been convinced by Lewis) proved that if, in a given belief state, there is a proposition A > B such that Prob(B given A) = Prob(A > B), then there exist, in the same belief state, two further propositions (compounds of A, B

---

[21] I use 'world' loosely, as a convenient short word for 'epistemic possibility'.

and A > B), C and D, such that Prob(D given C) ≠ Prob(C > D).[22] Perhaps we can still retain the Equation for propositions which do not have embedded conditionals, construing the proposition expressed as relative to a belief state. But the price is prohibitively high: we find that any difference or change of opinion about the likelihood that B if A, entails that a different proposition is under consideration.

## 5. *Possible Worlds*

I shall say little about Woods's careful and thorough exposition of possible-worlds semantics for counterfactuals. This discussion serves, in part, as a prelude to Woods's final section, in which he sketches a different account of counterfactuals. It is also relevant to the unfolding of the plot on Simple Conditionals, for some philosophers have argued that all conditionals can be given truth-conditions in terms of minimally different possible worlds.[23]

I shall make one comment on Woods's attitude to 'back-trackers': counterfactuals whose antecedent concerns a later time than the consequent. Lewis discusses these by reference to a puzzle of P. B. Downing's:[24] Jack and Jim, normally good friends, have quarrelled; Jack needs help; because of the quarrel, he does not ask Jim for help; and indeed, because of the quarrel,

(1) if Jack had asked Jim for help, Jim would not have obliged.

But alternatively, it could be argued, Jack would only have asked Jim for help if they had already made up the quarrel, in which case help would have been granted; so,

(2) if Jack had asked Jim for help, Jim would have obliged.

Note that the justification of (2) goes via a back-tracker. Lewis's

---

[22] See Bas van Fraassen, 'Probabilities of Conditionals', in W. Harper and C. Hooker (eds.), *Foundations of Probability Theory, Statistical Inference and Statistical Theories of Science*, i (Dordrecht, 1976), 303–4; Gibbard, 'Two Recent Theories of Conditionals', 219–20; and Edgington, 'On Conditionals', 276–8.

[23] See Stalnaker, 'A Theory of Conditionals' and 'Indicative Conditionals'; Davis, 'Indicative and Subjunctive Conditionals'.

[24] P. B. Downing, 'Subjunctive Conditionals, Time Order, and Causation', *Proceedings of the Aristotelian Society*, 59 (1958–9), 125–40.

response to the puzzle is as follows. Similarity between worlds is, admittedly, vague. On the standard resolution of vagueness, we keep the past in line—we consider worlds which do not differ from ours until immediately before the time when they must diverge to make the antecedent true. So, on our standard resolution of vagueness, (1) is true and (2) is false. But we can, on occasion, adopt a non-standard criterion of similarity, under which we accept (2). Lewis remarks on the fact that we tend to use a different form of words in our non-standard backwards counterfactual reasoning: we tend to say, 'If Jack had asked Jim for help, there would have had to have been no quarrel,' or perhaps, 'If Jack had asked Jim for help, that would have been because they had already made up their quarrel.'[25]

Woods is more antipathetic towards back-tracking counterfactuals than Lewis is. He calls them 'bizarre' (p. 51); and says 'we are not ready to consider how things would have been *earlier* if a certain counterfactual supposition had been fulfilled' (p. 52). He discusses Lewis's remark about the preferability of a different form of words for 'back-trackers': rather than saying:

(3) If he had arrived on time, he would have caught the train,

we prefer:

(4) If he had arrived on time, that could only have been because he caught the train,

or:

(5) If he had arrived on time, he would have had to have caught the train.

Woods comments

But the effect of such forms of words is to make the conditional not a back-tracking conditional after all. Such sentences do not say that if something had been the case at one time, something else would have been the case *earlier*; they say that if something had been the case, it would (then) have had a certain explanation, or that (then) something would have needed to have happened earlier. (p. 52)

However, if something is now explained by P, it had better be the

---

[25] Lewis, 'Counterfactual Dependence and Time's Arrow'.

case that P was true: (4) surely entails (3), and so does (5). 'If it had been the case that Q, that would have been because P' entails 'If it had been the case that Q, it would have been the case that P', as does 'If it had been the case that Q, it would have had to have been the case that P'. Woods's antipathy towards back-trackers seems too strong. Bennett points out that there is nothing bizarre about 'If Stevenson had been President in 1953, he would have won the election in 1952';[26] and some of Woods's examples are not that bizarre: 'If Jones had voted for the motion, he would have been at the meeting.'

Woods endorses Jackson's arguments against treating Simple Conditionals as possible-worlds conditionals.[27] And he shows that considerations of similarity between worlds seem to lead to wrong verdicts, for examples like 'If the accused is innocent, many of the witnesses are lying' and 'If the janitor was speaking the truth, no one left the building all night' (p. 54). One of Jackson's arguments is this: a possible-worlds analysis clearly allows the truth-value of a proposition B in the nearest A-world to be different from the truth-value of B in the actual world. Thus it fits counterfactuals of the form: 'If A had been true, such-and-such things would have been different from the way they actually are.' But there are no acceptable Simple Conditionals of the form 'If A is true, such-and-such things are different from the way they actually are'. If Simple Conditionals were possible-worlds conditionals, there would be acceptable instances of this form. Hence Simple Conditionals are not possible-world conditionals.

## 6. *Compounds*

In his sixth section Woods considers which account of Simple Conditionals best explains the behaviour of compounds of conditionals. He notes that if we deny truth-conditions to Simple Conditionals, we have no automatic way of explaining their occurrence in longer sentences (and quotes Lewis to this effect). On the other hand, if we do give them truth-conditions, the automatic ways of generating truth-conditions for longer sentences

[26] Bennett, 'Counterfactuals and Temporal Direction', 57.
[27] See Jackson, *Conditionals*, 70–6.

containing conditionals tend to give counterintuitive answers. This is well known if we give them truth-functional truth-conditions (as Lewis does), but it is also the case for non-truth-functional truth-conditions.

When he comes to consider the various kinds of sentence with conditional components, Woods is evidently doing creative work. He is not employing already-known principles for determining the content of, e.g., a disjunction, given the content of its disjuncts. He sees this section, then, as supporting the no-truth-value position.

Sentences of the form 'If A, then if B then C' he treats as equivalent to sentences of the form 'If A&B then C'. Thus, the embedded conditional may be explained away. I think he is correct, but will add two observations. First, the possible-worlds semantics of Stalnaker (and Lewis for counterfactuals) does not have this equivalence; for them, it may be true that if A&B then C, yet false that if A, then if B, C, and vice versa. Second, accepting the equivalence has the consequence that either *modus ponens* is not always valid for conditionals with conditional consequents, *or* the truth-functional account is correct.[28] Perhaps we can see this if we consider the trivial conditional 'If A&B then A'. This should be equivalent to 'If A, then if B then A'. So, with *modus ponens*, we may infer 'If B then A' from 'A'. Only the truth-functional conditional licenses this inference. (Of course, if you explain away the apparent conditional with conditional consequent as 'really' of the form 'If A&B then C', the problem with *modus ponens* does not arise.)

Next Woods considers a peculiarity of disjunctive antecedents: a sentence like 'If John is in Italy or in France, he is in Rome' can be highly acceptable, on the Ramsey–Adams account. Also, it can be true on the Stalnaker–Lewis account: the nearest world in which John is in Italy or in France, may be one in which he is in Rome. This is not obviously wrong: I am told that he is either in Italy or in France, and respond, 'Well, if he's in Italy or France, he's in Rome—that is the only place in Italy or France to which he ever goes.' Another example, from McKay and van Inwagen

---

[28] Vann McGee argues against *modus ponens* in cases like this: 'A Counter-example to Modus Ponens', *Journal of Philosophy*, 82 (1985), 462–71. Adams, *The Logic of Conditionals*, 33, noted the problem.

(this concerns a counterfactual, but the point could be transferred to a Simple Conditional):

> 'Which side did Spain fight on in the Second World War?'
> 'Neither—Spain didn't enter the war—but if she had fought on one side or the other, she would have fought on Germany's side.'[29]

But there is perhaps another way of parsing sentences like 'If I had had either Smith or Jones as a tutor, I would have passed' (again, the example could be transformed into a Simple Conditional): 'If A, or if B, then C'; i.e., 'whichever of A or B, then C'—as not of the form, 'If it had been (is) true that (A or B) it would have been (is) true that C'; but rather of the form, '(If A then C) and (if B then C).' McKay and van Inwagen point out that there are many non-conditional uses of 'or' for which thought is required in discerning their logical form: 'You can either fly or take the train.'

Disjunctions of conditionals Woods reinterprets as really no such thing. 'Either we'll have fish, if John arrives, or we'll have leftovers, if he doesn't.' This means: either we'll have fish or leftovers; if John arrives, we'll have fish; if John does not arrive, we'll have leftovers.[30]

It is very difficult to think of a context in which we would want genuinely to disjoin conditionals: to say something of the form, 'Either (if A, B), or (if C, D)—but I don't know which.' And it is very difficult to explain the absence of thoughts of this form, on the hypothesis that conditionals have truth-conditions. 'Or' is a very useful word, especially when it connects things we can be uncertain about, for we are often in a position to be confident that A or B, while not knowing which. We can be uncertain about conditionals. Yet thoughts of this form do not occur naturally. Of course, our ordinary need for disjunctions does show up inside conditionals: 'If A, then either B or C (I don't know which).'

With conditionals in antecedents, sentences of the form 'If (B

---

[29] Thomas McKay and Peter van Inwagen, 'Counterfactuals with Disjunctive Antecedents', *Philosophical Studies*, 31 (1977), 353–6.

[30] I used 'will' conditionals here, forgetting that they are to be left aside until the last section. I could easily have changed the example. But I decided to leave it, because it will be significant later that these points about compounds apply to conditionals of all forms.

if A), then C', the best we can do, Woods holds, is to discern, in the context of utterance, some obvious basis, D, for the assertion that if A, B; and construe the conditional as saying 'If D then C'. 'If the light goes on if you press the switch, the electrician has called'—'If the power is on, the electrician has called.' This was Gibbard's thought, and it is also endorsed by Jackson;[31] though they, more than Woods, highlight the tenuous and uncertain nature of this strategy. There is no guarantee that a hearer is able to identify, in context, an obvious basis for the assertion that if A, B; so some conditionals with conditional antecedents are uninterpretable. Gibbard gives the example, 'If Kripke was there if Strawson was there, then Anscombe was there.' But, being co-operative creatures, we do our best to interpret the remarks of our fellows, by *ad hoc* strategies, and do our best to come up with a likely hypothesis about what someone who utters a sentence of this form has in mind. Another interpretation is sometimes possible, suggested by Dummett.[32] You may be interpreted as saying 'If you accept that B if A, you must (surely) accept this': 'If John should be punished if he took the money, then Mary should be punished if she took the money.'

Negations of conditionals, Woods argues, can be understood in two ways. 'It is not the case that, if Jones was at the meeting, he voted for the proposal' may be read as 'If Jones was at the meeting, it's not the case that he voted for the proposal'. On the other hand, if I say, 'If you are over 65, you are entitled to a reduction,' and you respond, 'That's not true,' you may not be claiming that if you are over 65, you are not entitled to a reduction, but merely that it is far from certain that you are entitled to a reduction, if you are over 65. Compare the two ways in which one might disagree with an unconditional assertion, 'It will rain,' one stronger than the other: you may say 'No, it won't rain'; or you may say, 'I wouldn't be so sure.' Similarly, you can assert, deny, or express uncertainty about B, on the assumption that A, without ever using the negation of a whole conditional. We do not appear to have determined a univocal use for the latter—

---

[31] Gibbard, 'Two Recent Theories of Conditionals'; Jackson, *Conditionals*, 129–34.

[32] *Frege: The Philosophy of Language*, 351–4; see also Dummett, *The Logical Basis of Metaphysics* (London, 1992), 171–2.

which (as in the case of disjunctions) is surprising if conditionals have truth-conditions.

Along the way, Woods shows how counterintuitive embedded conditionals are when they are construed truth-functionally. For non-truth-functional truth-conditions also, disputes persist. Stalnaker asserts, and Lewis denies (for counterfactuals), the Law of Conditional Excluded Middle: Either (if A, B) or (if A, ¬B). Lewis admits that there is much to be said for the Law, but thinks there is more to be said against it—he calls it 'the principal virtue and the principal vice of Stalnaker's theory'.[33] These disputed issues about compounds of conditionals show that if conditionals do have truth-conditions, we are far from clear about which they are. The facts square at least as well with the hypothesis that conditionals do not have truth-conditions—some apparent embeddings of conditionals are explained away, as equivalent to sentences without such embeddings, others we do our best to interpret by *ad hoc* strategies.

## 7. *Other Conditional Speech Acts*

Woods adduces further evidence in favour of his view that Simple Conditionals are used to make conditional assertions, by considering commands and questions. As he commented at the beginning of his first section, it would be very implausible to deny that the 'If'-clause functions in a uniform way in, for example,

If John is in his office, he is working on his lecture;

If John is in his office, tell him to phone me;

If John is in his office, is he alone?

A theory of conditionals should be applicable to more than conditional statements—expressions of conditional beliefs.

This is quite a severe test. For example, neither the truth-functional account, nor Jackson's supplement to it, nor Stalnaker's possible-world account, extends plausibly to commands of conditional form. The doctor says to the nurse in the emergency ward:

---

[33] *Counterfactuals*, 79.

(*) 'If the patient is still alive in the morning, change the dressing.'

If we try to interpret (*) truth-functionally, we have to give the command wide scope: 'Either the patient will not be alive, or change the dressing' is not even grammatical. Giving the command wide scope, it would be equivalent to: 'Make it the case that either the patient is not alive in the morning, or the dressing is changed by you.' The nurse will obey *this* command if he holds a pillow over the patient's face.

Jackson claims that in asserting that 'If A, B' I assert that $\neg A \vee B$, and also indicate that my belief is robust with respect to the antecedent: learning that the antecedent is true would not make me abandon my belief. The parallel account of commands of conditional form would interpret the doctor as commanding the disjunction, and indicating that this command is robust with respect to the antecedent—the doctor would still issue the command if she knew the antecedent were true. This does not change the case significantly: the nurse still obeys the command if he kills the patient. There is no obvious reason why he should concern himself with the question what the doctor would have commanded in a different situation, rather than what she did command.

On a possible-worlds interpretation like Stalnaker's, (*) would seem to mean: 'In the nearest possible world to the actual world in which the patient is still alive in the morning, change the dressing.' Now suppose the nurse forgets all about the command, or alternatively has no inclination to obey it; but the patient dies before the night is through. On Stalnaker's analysis, the nurse disobeyed the order (for, in the nearest possible world in which the patient was alive, he did not change the dressing). Similarly, on Stalnaker's account, I could break my promise to go to the doctor if the pain gets worse, even if the pain gets better. This is wrong: conditional commands and promises are not requirements on my behaviour in other possible worlds.

It is more natural to give a uniform account of conditional speech acts, as having the force of a command, assertion, etc., of the consequent in the event that the antecedent is true. Michael Dummett has objected to this idea, however:[34] for commands

---

[34] Dummett, 'Truth', 8–9; *Frege: Philosophy of Language*, 340; *The Logical Basis of Metaphysics*, 115.

and assertions of conditional form, it is unacceptable to say that if the antecedent proves false, it is as if nothing has been said. I say, 'If you press that switch, there will be an explosion.' Consequently, you do not press it. Had I said nothing at all, let us suppose you would have pressed it. A disaster is avoided, as a result of this piece of linguistic communication. It is not as though nothing has been said. Dummett's original example of a conditional command was, 'If you go out, wear your coat.' The child cannot find his coat, so stays in, in order not to disobey the command. Again, it is not as though nothing has been said.

But it is consistent to maintain that no (categorical) assertion was made, no command has been given, without maintaining that it is as though nothing has been said. Suppose you understand 'If you press the switch there will be an explosion' as a conditional assertion of the consequent. You realize that if you press it, my assertion will have categorical force; and, given that you take me to be trustworthy and reliable, if it does have categorical force, it is likely to be true. So you acquire a reason to think that there will be an explosion if you press the switch, and hence a reason not to press it. In the case of the command, if the child can't find his coat, he has a choice between going out and hence disobeying the command, or behaving in such a way that no (categorical) command has been given (not: behaving in such a way as though nothing has been said).

Woods discerns two kinds of conditional questions: those in which the speaker is asked to suppose that P, and say whether or not he accepts Q, on that supposition: 'If it rains, will the match be cancelled?'; and those in which the question lapses if the antecedent proves false: 'If you have been to London, did you like it?' Perhaps this difference reduces to the difference between the case in which the addressee is presumed to know the truth-value of the antecedent, and the case in which he is not presumed to know this. In the latter case, he is asked to suppose that the antecedent is true and give his conditional verdict about the consequent. In the former, if he knows that the antecedent is true, he is being asked the truth-value of the consequent. If he is sure that the antecedent is false, there is no conditional belief for him to express—the question lapses.

Woods had intended to add a discussion of 'even if' and 'only if' to this section. I shall not try to guess what he would have said, except to say that it would be in the spirit of his work to try to show that these are products of the general meaning of 'if' and the use of 'even' and 'only', in non-conditional contexts.

## 8. *Non-Simple Conditionals*

Woods's final section, 'Sketch of a Theory of "Counterfactual" Conditionals', is the most novel and intriguing part of the work. It is undoubtedly a sketch, more tentative and less complete than the rest. As we saw in Section 1, his aim is to show that 'counterfactuals' are to be understood in terms of the meaning of 'if' as it occurs in Simple Conditionals, together with the effect of the past tense, and of expressions like 'would'.

'If he came now, he would be very surprised,' he says, reports precisely what would have been reported yesterday by an utterance of 'If he comes tomorrow he will be very surprised': a sentence containing 'would' is the past tense of a sentence containing 'will'. This thesis has become popular through Dudman's work, and it is also found in Ernest Adams, Brian Skyrms, Brian Ellis, and other earlier writings.[35] If this thought is right, 'would'-conditionals are not simply of the 'If . . . then . . .' form, as they involve the application of the past tense to another conditional. The key to understanding 'woulds' then, is a theory of 'will'-conditionals, which have not entered the story so far.

What, Woods asks, are we to make of the present tense in the antecedent of sentences like 'If it rains this afternoon, the match will be cancelled'? It is not simply an idiosyncratic quirk, for some antecedents do require 'will'. Compare 'If she receives the letter tomorrow, she will be in a bad mood' and 'If she will receive the letter tomorrow (anyway), I shall warn her about it today'. Dudman's example: 'If Granny will be dead by sundown we can start selling her clothes right now.'

---

[35] See Adams, *The Logic of Conditionals*, ch. 4; Skyrms, 'The Prior Propensity Account of Subjunctive Conditionals'; Brian Ellis, 'Two Theories of Indicative Conditionals', *Australasian Journal of Philosophy*, 62 (1984), 50–66. Adams (114–15) gave the example of the (rather wooden) argument: 'They will be here by eight; if they are here by eight we will eat at nine; so we will eat at nine,' being rephrased hungrily at ten: 'They should have been here by eight; if they had been here by eight, we would have eaten at nine; so we should have eaten at nine.'

These examples suggest that we get the present-tense antecedent when the conditional's consequent concerns a time later
than the antecedent's time. On this suggestion, it is not too difficult to rationalize the present-tense antecedent. Take a claim
about the future, 'It will rain this afternoon.' Now take a conditional claim about the future, 'It will rain this afternoon if the
wind doesn't change': the present-tense conditional clause is a
convenient way of indicating on what *earlier* condition I assert
that it will rain. Woods endorses this suggestion. Comparing 'If
it rains this afternoon, the match will be cancelled' and 'If it will
rain this afternoon, the match will be cancelled', he says that the
first 'implies, as the [second] does not, that the cancellation
occurs *after* the [hypothesized] occurrence of rain' (p. 80).

Unfortunately, this suggestion is not invariably correct: there
are present-tense antecedents whose consequents concern an
earlier time: 'If Granny goes to the dentist tomorrow, she will
clean her teeth beforehand'; 'If I kill myself, I'll kill you first'
(Dudman's examples). (Also the two clauses may be simultane-
ous: 'If he's not at home by eight, he will be working late in the
office.') These examples cast doubt on Woods's claim about 'If it
rains this afternoon, the match will be cancelled'. If the match is
cancelled when the storm clouds gather, but before the rain
begins, I don't think this conditional claim has been refuted.

The conditionals with 'will' in the antecedent are the rare
exceptions. One hypothesis, which fits the above examples about
the letter and Granny's imminent death, is that they be read 'If it
is now determined that such-and-such will happen . . .'. If this
hypothesis is correct, the following should be glaringly obvious:
'If Mary will win the lottery, there are corrupt practices
involved.' It is not glaringly obvious to me that that is glaringly
obvious, nor that 'If Mary will win the lottery, she will do so
against the odds' is obviously wrong.

If there is something systematic to be discovered here, it is un-
clear what. It is worth noting the different grammatical behaviour
of two factive alternatives to 'If', 'Since', and 'When'. We have
'Since it will rain tomorrow . . .' but 'When it rains tomorrow . . .'.
('Because' is like 'Since': 'Because it will rain tomorrow . . . .'
'Until' is like 'When': 'The grass will stay brown until it rains.')
But this observation fails to illuminate 'If'. Consider 'If he wins
the nomination, he will win the election'. Its factive, more up-beat

version is 'Since he will win the nomination, he will win the election', not 'When he wins the nomination, he will win the election'. Our first attempted explanation of the present-tense antecedent may still elucidate the central case, for 'will' conditionals. Not being in a position to say categorically whether it will rain, I say 'If the wind doesn't change, it will rain'. What will happen depends (causally) upon what happens earlier, and this is conveniently indicated by the tense of the antecedent. Perhaps the exceptions to the temporal asymmetry are merely an extension of a grammatical feature beyond the central cases which give it its rationale.

Here is Woods's proposal about the logical form of sentences like 'If he catches the train, he will arrive in time':

> They are best understood as containing an application of the present-tense 'will' to a sentence or predicate[36] that is already of the 'If . . . then . . .' form. If so, the final sentence will not itself be of that form. The 'If . . . then . . .' construction is the same, semantically, as the one we find in sentences of the 'If . . . then . . .' form built up from two arbitrary sentences. (pp. 81–2)

Thus we have something of the form 'Will (If John catches the train, John arrives on time)' (p. 82). What semantic function does 'will' perform?

> I suggest that [its] purport . . . is something like the following: 'Matters are (now) such as to ground an assertion of "If P then Q", where this is a matter of the *objective* probability of Q, given P—what would be assertible from an ideal epistemic standpoint.' If we want to sum up what is reported in the present by 'will', and in the past by 'would', we could say it is the presence of a tendency or disposition. If it is true that if it rains the match will be cancelled, matters are so disposed as to ensure cancellation in the event of rain. But exactly *what* is reported by 'will' will vary as much from case to case as the circumstances in which a Simple Conditional is assertible . . . The effect of putting the conditional judgement within the scope of 'will' is to de-relativize the

---

[36] 'Predicate' because it might be an open sentence, bound by a quantifier with wider scope than 'will'; see Woods's footnote on pp. 82–3, which makes a subtle point about scope. We need to be able to give two readings of 'If we run out of beer, someone will go out and buy some more'. Dudman's construal of the grammatical structure permits only one reading.

judgement, so that its assertibility turns on the *objective* probability of Q
given P, and not the speaker's subjective epistemic position. (pp. 83–4)

All that is quite something for 'will' to do!

Woods's overall picture, then, is this. Simple Conditionals are
used to make conditional assertions, to express conditional
beliefs, beliefs under a supposition. (There are also conditional
commands, questions, etc.) Sometimes, in order to understand a
longer sentence in which a Simple Conditional is embedded, we
need to identify, with the help of the context, a proposition which
is the ground that would justify the conditional assertion, and
which gives the conditional a sort of context-dependent truth-
condition. One kind of embedding is within a tense-operator.
Take 'If it had rained, the match would have been cancelled'. A
conditional occurs within a past-tense operator. It says something like 'Matters were such as to ground an assertion that the
match be cancelled, conditional upon rain'. It is a past-tense version of a conditional like 'If it rains, the match will be cancelled'.
The latter, then, says something like 'Matters *are* such as to
ground an assertion that the match will be cancelled, conditional
upon rain'. In the latter, 'will' has wider scope than 'if'. (An analogy is drawn with 'necessarily' or 'certainly' occurring in consequents.) 'Will' is present tense. Its function is to objectify, to
de-relativize the conditional judgement. For such conditionals
'there is no reason to doubt that they are made true by what is
actually the case' (p. 90).

Several questions arise about this theory of 'will'-conditionals.
First, Woods seems undecided between two theses: (A) that a
'will'-conditional requires that matters be such that the
antecedent *ensures* the truth of the consequent; (B) that a 'will'-
conditional requires that the objective probability of consequent
given antecedent be high. On (A), the objective probability of Q
given P may be 99 per cent, yet the corresponding 'will'-condi-
tional false: matters are not now such that P *ensures* the truth of
Q. If (B) is intended, there may indeed be objectively correct current opinions about whether if P, Q; but truth-conditions are still
problematic, *pace* Woods (p. 90). Suppose I know that the objective probability of Q given P is 99 per cent, and am therefore 99
per cent confident that Q if P. What I know to obtain is not
enough for the conditional to be true: if it were, I would be cer-

tain that it is true, and hence be 100 per cent confident that if P, Q. Nor is it enough for the conditional to be false: if it were, I should be certain that it is false, and hence be zero per cent confident that if P, Q. Objective probabilities may ground objectively right opinions, yet not yield truth-values for conditionals. To illustrate with a simple numerical example: you are about to pick a ball at random from a bag, and 90 per cent of the red balls have black spots. Knowing this, you are 90 per cent confident that if you pick a red ball, it will have a black spot. The aforementioned conditional is not known to be true, nor is it known to be false, nor does it express some proposition which is 90 per cent likely to be true—for conditional probabilities are not the probabilities of the truth of any proposition.

Secondly, let us consider Woods's claim that 'will' is present-tense. There is indeed a present-tense 'will', which indicates that you are *inferring*, rather than observing, something about the present. Dudman points this out by comparing 'The washing is dry now' and 'The washing will be dry now'. But in the class of conditionals we are considering, it seems more natural to take 'will' as indicating that the consequent concerns the future: there is the non-conditional assertion 'He will be home by six', and the qualified, conditional assertion 'If he catches the four o'clock train, he will be home by six'. It is difficult to find anything other than a temporal difference between:

(1) If he caught the ten o'clock train, he arrived at noon;

(2) If he caught the eleven o'clock train, he will arrive at one;

(3) If he catches the twelve o'clock train, he will arrive at two.

Thirdly, consider Woods's claim that the assertibility of such a conditional 'turns on the *objective* probability of Q, given P, and not the speaker's subjective epistemic position'. How can the assertibility of anything not turn on the speaker's subjective epistemic position? I take Woods to mean that it does not turn only on this: it is not enough, for the assertion of a 'will'-conditional, to have a high degree of confidence in consequent given antecedent; you must also believe that the consequent is objectively probable, given the antecedent: that there is, independently of your epistemic state, a high chance of Q given P.

Here is an example of the 'person-relative' kind of ground on which one sometimes accepts a Simple Conditional. I hear the foreman tell someone to fetch the hammer. There are three workmen around, but I have information sufficient to eliminate Jack—he was not the one spoken to. 'If he didn't tell Fred, he told Bob,' I conclude. Knowing that each is obedient, can I not further conclude that if Fred doesn't fetch the hammer, Bob will fetch it? Objective probabilities do not arise here. Consider another observer who also heard the foreman's order, and has information sufficient to eliminate Bob. 'If Fred doesn't fetch the hammer, Jack will fetch it,' she thinks. The objective probability that Bob will fetch it given that Fred doesn't, and the objective probability that Jack will fetch it given that Fred doesn't, can't both be high. I concede that these are not the most typical grounds for 'will'-conditionals, but the conditionals are not obviously unacceptable.

I agree with Woods on the relation between 'woulds' and 'wills', and on his account of Simple Conditionals, but I am unconvinced by his distancing of 'will'-conditionals from Simple Conditionals. Much of his earlier discussion of Simple Conditionals applies also to 'wills'. Consider conditional commands and questions. The most common conditional commands have antecedents suited to 'will'-conditionals: 'If you go out tonight, wear your coat'; 'If the patient is still alive in the morning, change the dressing.' If any sentences are to be construed as commanding the consequent conditionally upon the antecedent's being true, these are. And conditional questions: 'If it rains, will the match be cancelled?' 'If John comes to your party tonight, how will you avoid a fight?' It is, as we saw, obligatory that we give a uniform account of a conditional clause like 'If he phones' in:

If he phones, Mary will be pleased.

If he phones, what shall I say?

If he phones, hang up immediately.

We do so if we construe the first as a conditional assertion of 'Mary will be pleased'.

Next consider compounds. Woods's point about the non-standard interpretation of disjunctions of conditionals is just as persuasive when the disjoined conditionals are 'wills'. I gave an example on p. 122. Conditionals in antecedents are still to be interpreted *ad hoc*, negations of conditionals are still ambiguous. It is hard to explain why this should be so if, as Woods says of 'wills', 'there is no reason for denying that they are made true by what is actually the case' (p. 90).

Further, the Ramsey–Adams account of degree of conditional belief is as plausible for 'will'-conditionals as it is for any: I accept 'If it rains, the match will be cancelled' to the extent that I think it is probable that the match will be cancelled (C), on the supposition that it rains (R). This is equivalent to judging (R&C) much more likely than (R&¬C). So, *ceteris paribus*, I am prepared to assert that it will be cancelled, conditionally upon its raining.

Woods gives a tricky example designed to show that the Ramsey–Adams account can fail for some forward-looking conditionals. The question arises whether Jones will apply for the job, and whether he will be successful if he does so. I know that Jones would not apply without encouragement from those offering the job; and that they would not encourage him to apply unless they were virtually certain to offer him the job if he did apply. Do I, or do I not, accept as probable, 'If he applies, he will get the job'? Do I, or do I not, at a later time (with no new information), accept as probable, 'If he applied, he got the job'? Woods answers 'No' to the first question and 'Yes' to the second. It seems to me that the answer is less clear—we could go either way—as it is unclear which of two situations we are supposing to obtain when we make the supposition. It is not obviously wrong to argue, 'If he applies, he will get the job; for he won't apply unless he is invited to apply; and he won't be invited to apply unless he is virtually certain to be offered the job if he applies.' In any case there are innumerable cases in which the Ramsey–Adams account is as good for 'will'-conditionals as it is for any. To repeat a toy example, suppose that 90 per cent of the red balls in the bag have a black spot. How confident should you be that if you pick a red ball, it will have a black spot?

Woods's account of 'will'-conditionals is motivated by the thought that more objectivity is typically available for them than for Simple Conditionals. I think this thought is correct, but it is to be explained by asymmetries in our epistemic access to the past and the future, which in turn relate to metaphysical asymmetries of dependence. I do not think this difference needs to be registered in a different logical form or semantics for these future-looking conditional sentences.

What is available to be discovered about the past is vast, what any individual knows is relatively small and idiosyncratic. The individual's use of Simple Conditionals reflects his particular combination of knowledge and ignorance. What is available to be discovered about the future is relatively little, and our methods for predicting the future relatively uniform and communal (we also defer to experts a good deal). Consider Woods's device of the 'ideal epistemic perspective'. This is elucidated in terms of someone who knows all he needs to know about the past and present, and the laws of nature, to assess a given conditional. Call him G. Now G knows too much to have any interest in a Simple Conditional about the present or past, for he knows the truthvalues of antecedent and consequent. He knows that A&B or knows that A&¬B or knows that ¬A. In the first two cases he can pronounce the conditional trivially true or false. In the third case the question doesn't arise. Such conditionals are helpful tools for managing ignorance: no ignorance, no use.

What about forward-looking conditionals? The answer depends on the structure of the laws with which our ideal knower is equipped. If determinism is true and we give our ideal knower all the deterministic laws he needs, he is as well-placed with respect to the future as he is with respect to the past. For future A and B, he will know their truth-values. If A is false, the past and the laws will tell him that ¬A, the question what will be true if A is true does not arise. Suppose however that determinism is false; or that it is true but we prefer to think of even our idealized knower as, like us, needing probabilistic laws. This is to give G a future of forking paths, to which probabilities can be attached. Then there can be objectively best estimates of the probability of B given A for our ideal knower to make, and for us to aim at.

(Interestingly, for there to be non-trivial objectively correct future-looking conditional judgements, we need undetermined antecedents (or need to idealize at a level at which there are undetermined antecedents). It follows that there will also be undetermined consequents, and our best conditional judgements will be probabilistic.)

G's judgements of conditional and unconditional probability

will change with time, according to the outcomes of intervening chance events. The probability of my winning my bet on three heads is $\frac{1}{8}$. After the first toss, it has changed to either $\frac{1}{4}$ or $0$, for the probability of $\frac{1}{2}$ that the first toss *had* of landing heads has now 'collapsed' to either $1$ or $0$. On Monday it is objectively probable that the patient will survive if we operate on Friday. Then something improbable happens, and it is no longer probable that she will survive if we operate. Eventually the future becomes past, and the conditional becomes redundant for G, who knows the truth-values of its parts. (Thus, objectively correct probability judgements are transient, unlike truth-values.) Leaving G behind, our epistemic degrees of belief are the best estimates we are able to make of objective chances, when such there be. They too change with time and the acquisition of new information. It *was* improbable that I *would* win the lottery. But now I have good evidence that I have won. So we can understand the 'would'-judgements, as our best present estimates of how likely something *was*, or how likely something was given something else, in an earlier situation. The 'wills' and the Simple Conditionals, on the other hand, are assessed relative to our present epistemic state. Relative to my present epistemic state, I am sure that someone else killed Kennedy, on the supposition that Oswald didn't. That leaves me free to judge (thinking as I do that Oswald did it), that it was improbable that anyone else would if he hadn't—my present estimate of how the probabilities lay, at a time before the killing, endorses the judgement that would have been made then by the words 'If Oswald doesn't kill him, no one else will'.

Thus, I am in substantial agreement with Woods, despite disagreeing with his analysis of 'will'-conditionals. I also think he is right to suggest that 'further out' counterfactuals can be understood by analogy to the standard, past-tense ones. With the standard ones, you adopt, hypothetically, an epistemic perspective different from your actual one, which you take to be suited to some time in the past, a time when the antecedent was (you think) a live possibility. Other cases can also be seen as adopting an epistemic perspective, different from your actual one, in which the antecedent is an epistemic possibility, but not necessarily one which you think it would ever be right to take as a live possibility. 'If the square root of 2 were rational, then . . .' is an example.

Woods raised earlier (Section 5) a worry about whether the possible-worlds semantics can explain the point of counterfactual judgements—why they matter to us. Why should we be interested in what goes on in similar possible worlds? 'I want to be told something about this world, not some other possible world, when I ask whether, if she hadn't been given that drug, she would have survived.' It is not clear that the worry is well founded. Which worlds are 'similar', in the required respects, to this one, depends on what this world is like. So you do learn what this world is like, if you are told that one like it but for the difference required by her not taking the drug, is one in which she survived. The thought might remain, though, that if important information about this world is conveyed by counterfactuals, it should be possible to represent this information in a more direct, less fanciful way.

To assess this issue would involve a careful examination of the serious use we make of counterfactual judgements, in questions that matter to us, and which theories properly account for the significance of this use. We use them a great deal in empirical inference—in the attempt to draw true conclusions about this world.[37] There is the 'counterfactual *modus tollens*' style of inference: 'They're not at home; for the lights are off; and if they had been at home the lights would have been on.' And there is the 'inference to the best explanation' style of reasoning, which I mentioned in my first section: 'He jumped from that window; for the plants are damaged; and they would be damaged if he had jumped from there.' 'I think she took arsenic; for she has symptoms X, Y, and Z, and these are just the symptoms she would have if she had taken arsenic.' The matter requires detailed investigation, which I will not pursue, save to say that the probabilistic approach to counterfactuals fits well-known models of empirical reasoning about this world. Woods rather underestimates the importance of counterfactuals, saying that it is understandable that we should be interested in them 'even though that interest is not a practical one'. An interest in discovering what is true is often a 'practical' interest, and counterfactual judgements are needed in this endeavour.

Woods's careful and thought-provoking essay has been of great benefit to me. The substantial point upon which we dis-

---

[37] See Adams, 'On The Rightness of Certain Counterfactuals', *Pacific Philosophical Quarterly*, 74 (1993), 1–10.

agree—the treatment of 'wills'—is small compared with the extent to which I think he is right. I have learned much, and thought much, about conditionals as a result of reading his work.

I hope and expect that his essay will induce others to new thoughts and further work on this important and intractable topic.

# WORKS CITED

Adams, Ernest. 'On the Logic of Conditionals', *Inquiry*, 8 (1965), 166–97.

—— 'On the Rightness of Certain Counterfactuals', *Pacific Philosophical Quarterly*, 74 (1993), 1–10.

—— 'Probability and the Logic of Conditionals', in J. Hintikka and P. Suppes (eds.), *Aspects of Inductive Logic* (Amsterdam: North-Holland, 1966), 256–316.

—— 'Subjunctive and Indicative Conditionals', *Foundations of Language*, 6 (1970), 89–94.

—— *The Logic of Conditionals* (Dordrecht: Reidel, 1975).

Anderson, Alan Ross. 'A Note on Subjunctive and Counterfactual Conditionals', *Analysis*, 12 (1951), 35–8.

Appiah, A. *Assertion and Conditionals* (Cambridge: Cambridge University Press, 1985).

Bayes, Thomas. 'An Essay Towards Solving a Problem in the Doctrine of Chances', in W. E. Deming (ed.), *Facsimiles of Two Papers by Bayes* (Washington, DC: US Department of Agriculture, 1940). (Originally published in *Transactions of the Royal Society of London*, 53 (1763), 370–418.)

Bennett, Jonathan. 'Counterfactuals and Temporal Direction', *Philosophical Review*, 93 (1984), 57–91.

—— 'Farewell to the Phlogiston Theory of Conditionals', *Mind*, 97 (1988), 509–27.

Carnap, Rudolf. 'Testability and Meaning', *Philosophy of Science*, 3 (1936), 419–71; 4 (1937), 1–40.

Chisholm, R. M. 'The Contrary-to-Fact Conditional', *Mind*, 55 (1946), 289–307.

Cohen, L. J. 'Some Remarks on Grice's Views about the Logical Particles of Natural Language', in Y. Bar-Hillel (ed.), *The Pragmatics of Natural Languages* (Dordrecht: Reidel, 1971), 50–68.

Davidson, Donald. 'Mental Events', *Essays on Actions and Events* (Oxford: Clarendon Press, 1980), 207-25.

—— 'The Logical Form of Action Sentences', *Essays on Actions and Events* (Oxford: Clarendon Press, 1980), 105–22.

Davis, Wayne A. 'Indicative and Subjunctive Conditionals', *Philosophical Review*, 88 (1979), 544–64.

Downing, P. B. 'Subjunctive Conditionals, Time Order, and Causation', *Proceedings of the Aristotelian Society*, 59 (1958–9), 125–40.

Dudman, V. H. 'Appiah on "If"', *Analysis*, 47 (1987), 74–9.

—— 'Conditional Interpretations of "If"-Sentences', *Australian Journal of Linguistics*, 4 (1984), 143–204.

——'Indicative and Subjunctive', *Analysis*, 48 (1988), 113–22.

—— 'Parsing "If"-Sentences', *Analysis*, 44 (1984), 145–53.

—— 'Tense and Time in English Verb Clusters of the Primary Pattern', *Australian Journal of Linguistics*, 3 (1983), 35–44.

—— 'Vive la Revolution!', *Mind*, 98 (1989), 591–603.

Dummett, Michael. *Frege: The Philosophy of Language* (London: Duckworth, 1973).

—— *The Logical Basis of Metaphysics* (London: Duckworth, 1992).

—— 'Truth', *Proceedings of the Aristotelian Society*, 59 (1958–9), 141–62; reprinted in *Truth and Other Enigmas* (q.v.), 1–24.

—— *Truth and Other Enigmas* (London: Duckworth, 1978).

Edgington, Dorothy. 'Do Conditionals Have Truth-Conditions?', *Crítica*, 18, No. 52 (1986), 3–30; reprinted in Frank Jackson (ed.), *Conditionals* (q.v.), 176–201.

—— 'On Conditionals', *Mind*, 104 (1995), 235–329.

—— 'The Mystery of the Missing Matter of Fact', *Proceedings of the Aristotelian Society Supplementary Volume*, 65 (1991), 185–209.

Ellis, Brian. 'Two Theories of Indicative Conditionals', *Australasian Journal of Philosophy*, 62 (1984), 50–66.

Gibbard, Allan. 'Two Recent Theories of Conditionals', in W. L. Harper, R. Stalnaker, and G. Pearce (eds.), *Ifs* (q.v.), 211–47.

Goodman, Nelson. *Fact, Fiction, and Forecast*, 4th edn. (Cambridge, Mass.: Harvard University Press, 1983).

—— 'The Problem of Counterfactual Conditionals', *Journal of Philosophy*, 44 (1947), 113–28; reprinted in Frank Jackson (ed.), *Conditionals* (q.v.), 9–27.

Grandy, R. E. and Warner, R. (eds.). *Philosophical Grounds of Rationality* (Oxford: Clarendon Press, 1986).

Grice, H. P. William James Lectures, in *Studies in the Way of Words* (Cambridge, Mass.: Harvard University Press, 1989).

Hare, R. M. 'Meaning and Speech Acts', *Philosophical Review*, 79 (1970), 3–24.

Harper, W. L. and Hooker, C. A. (eds.). *Foundations of Probability Theory, Statistical Inference, and Statistical Theories of Science*, vol. i (Dordrecht: Reidel, 1976).

Harper, W. L., Stalnaker, R., and Pearce, G. (eds.). *Ifs* (Dordrecht: Reidel, 1981).

Jackson, Frank. *Conditionals* (Oxford: Blackwell, 1987).

—— 'Conditionals and Possibilia', *Proceedings of the Aristotelian Society*, 81 (1980–1), 125–37.

—— 'On Assertion and Indicative Conditionals', *Philosophical Review*, 88 (1979), 565–89; reprinted in Frank Jackson (ed.), *Conditionals* (q.v.), 111–35.

—— (ed.). *Conditionals* (Oxford: Oxford University Press, 1991).

Lewis, David. *Counterfactuals* (Oxford: Blackwell, 1973).

—— 'Counterfactual Dependence and Time's Arrow', *Noûs*, 13 (1979), 455–76; reprinted in *Philosophical Papers*, vol. ii (q.v.), 32–66, and in Frank Jackson (ed.), *Conditionals* (q.v.), 46–75.

—— *Philosophical Papers*, vol. ii (New York: Oxford University Press, 1986).

—— 'Probabilities of Conditionals and Conditional Probabilities', *Philosophical Review*, 85 (1976), 297–315; reprinted in *Philosophical Papers*, vol. ii (q.v.), 133–52, in W. L. Harper, R. Stalnaker, and G. Pearce (eds.), *Ifs* (q.v.), 129–47, and in Frank Jackson (ed.), *Conditionals* (q.v.), 76–101.

—— 'Probabilities of Conditionals and Conditional Probabilities II', *Philosophical Review*, 5 (1986), 581–9; reprinted in Frank Jackson (ed.), *Conditionals* (q.v.), 102–10.

McGee, Vann. 'A Counterexample to Modus Ponens', *Journal of Philosophy*, 82 (1985), 462–71.

McKay, Thomas, and van Inwagen, Peter. 'Counterfactuals with Disjunctive Antecedents', *Philosophical Studies*, 31 (1977), 353–6.

Mackie, J. *Truth, Probability, and Paradox* (Oxford: Clarendon Press, 1973).

Mellor, D. H. 'How to Believe a Conditional', *Journal of Philosophy*, 90, No. 5 (1993), 233–48.

Quine, W. V. O. *Methods of Logic*, 3rd edn. (London: Routledge, 1974).

Ramsey, F. P. *The Foundations of Mathematics* (London: Routledge, 1931).

—— 'General Propositions and Causality', in *The Foundations of Mathematics* (q.v.), 237–55.

—— 'Truth and Probability', in *The Foundations of Mathematics* (q.v.), 156–98.

Ryle, Gilbert. '"If", "So", and "Because"', in Max Black (ed.), *Philosophical Analysis* (Englewood Cliffs, NJ: Prentice-Hall, 1950), 323–40.

Sanford, David. *If P, then Q: Conditionals and the Foundations of Reasoning* (London: Routledge, 1989).

Skyrms, B. 'The Prior Propensity Account of Subjunctive Conditionals', in W. L. Harper, R. Stalnaker, and G. Pearce (eds.), *Ifs* (q.v.), 259–65.

Smiley, Timothy. 'Hunter on Conditionals', *Proceedings of the Aristotelian Society*, 84 (1983–4), 241–9.

Stalnaker, Robert. 'A Theory of Conditionals', *Studies in Logical Theory*, American Philosophical Quarterly Monograph Series, No. 2 (Oxford: Blackwell, 1968), 98–112; reprinted in W. L. Harper, R. Stalnaker, and G. Pearce (eds.), *Ifs* (q.v.), 41–55, and in Frank Jackson (ed.), *Conditionals* (q.v.), 28–45.

—— 'Indicative Conditionals', *Philosophia*, 5 (1975), 269–86; reprinted in W. L. Harper, R. Stalnaker, and G. Pearce (eds.), *Ifs* (q.v.), 193–210, and in Frank Jackson (ed.), *Conditionals* (q.v.), 136–54.

Strawson, P. F. '"If" and "⊃"', in R. E. Grandy and R. Warner (eds.), *Philosophical Grounds of Rationality* (Oxford: Clarendon Press, 1986), 229–42.

—— *Introduction to Logical Theory* (London: Methuen, 1952).

Thomson, J. F. 'In Defense of ⊃', *Journal of Philosophy*, 87 (1990), 56–70.

van Fraassen, Bas. 'Probabilities of Conditionals', in W. Harper and C. Hooker (eds.), *Foundations of Probability Theory, Statistical Inference, and Statistical Theories of Science* (q.v.), 261–308.

von Wright, G. H. *Logical Studies* (London: Routledge, 1957).

# MICHAEL JOHN WOODS
## 1934–1993

## *John Ackrill*

The very first philosophy essay that Michael Woods wrote as an undergraduate of Brasenose College, Oxford—an essay on Mill's *Utilitarianism*—revealed his aptitude for the subject. It was clearly written and well argued, and in the discussion he was quick at grasping difficult points. He was evidently going to *enjoy* philosophy.

It was as a Classical scholar that Woods had come up (in 1953), and he had worked for Classical Honour Moderations under Maurice Platnauer. Fortunately, the Greats syllabus contained a large component of Greek philosophy, and Woods could combine his classical and philosophical interests in studying Plato's *Republic* and Aristotle's *Ethics*. It was no surprise that after taking a First in Greats he should go on to read for the B.Phil. (under the genial supervision of Henry Price), and that after a Senior Scholarship at Merton he should go on to a research and teaching post at Christ Church. In 1961, he was elected to an official fellowship as a philosophy tutor at Brasenose, where he remained until his death.

Michael Woods taught for most of the philosophy papers taken by undergraduates, and he was an excellent tutor. Stimulating the stronger pupil with difficult challenges, he could encourage and help the weaker pupil with clear explanations. Many of his pupils went on to further work in philosophy; most of them became and remained his friends.

Woods's own work in modern philosophy was mainly in philosophical logic and metaphysics. The many papers he published are clever and sometimes intricate, lucid and often highly illuminating. Numerous other papers were written for reading to seminars, discussion groups, or conferences. For he was always glad to accept invitations to perform on such occasions. He could be relied on to provoke and sustain lively and interesting discussion. His death prevents the completion of the book on philosophical logic on which he had been working in recent years.

In ancient philosophy Woods made notable contribution in papers on Plato's *Republic* and Aristotle's ethics and metaphysics. He also produced (in 1982) a book that will be used and valued as long as Aristotle is studied. The *Eudemian Ethics* is a work whose importance and interest have only lately been recognized; and there was no satisfactory English translation and no philosophical commentary at all until Woods's volume in the Clarendon Aristotle series. This was a task calling for meticulous Classical scholarship—the Greek text is in many places difficult or corrupt—and for acute philosophical analysis. Woods's volume moved the study of *Eudemian Ethics* on to a new level.

In 1992 a second edition was published, which took account of the new Oxford Classical text of 1991. Most of the work for this edition was done during a sabbatical year at the National Humanities Center in North Carolina. Woods greatly enjoyed this year (as he had enjoyed earlier sabbaticals at the universities of Minnesota and Cornell), and he took advantage of the opportunity to travel in the US and to meet friends and colleagues. He was always a great traveller. Holidays were usually taken on the Continent, most often in France or Italy. Alone or in company, by train or by bicycle, he relished the travelling, the art and architecture, the food and wine, the people to be visited.

The college was, however, the centre of his life. For many years he had a splendid set of rooms in the Old Quad. There he taught, worked, listened to music (especially opera), and entertained. He entertained generously and thoughtfully, and made a great contribution to the social cohesion of the college. His gift for sociability had full scope during his years as Curator of the Senior Common Room. Here, as in the college, he was always a unifying influence, promoting agreement and harmony.

Though Woods was not by nature an administrator, he took on many administrative duties for the college and the faculty. He was Vice-Principal for two busy years, covering the transition from one principal to another. He was for many years on the Faculty Board and the Philosophy Panel. He served on numerous committees: his experience, judgement, impartiality, and good humour made him invaluable.

Woods saw great changes in college and university life. The size of the college grew, women were admitted, organization and administration became more complex, the style of life of the undergraduates changed. All this he took in his stride. Though mildly conservative by temperament, he was very liberal in his views and not given to nostalgia. The introduction of a computer into his study might have been expected to disconcert a Classical scholar with no pretension to technical skill or scientific expertise. In fact, Woods was delighted with his computer—pleased and somewhat amused to find that he could use it to very good effect.

A few years ago he moved from his resident's rooms in college to a comfortable and convenient town-house, an easy walk or cycle ride from college (where he continued to have rooms for teaching and research).

Michael Woods was liked and trusted by everybody. He had a fine sense of humour and great *joie de vivre*. He did well in all his roles: as tutor, philosopher, colleague, friend. He will be remembered with deep affection.

Reprinted by permission from the *Independent*, Obituaries, 12 April 1993.

# CURRICULUM VITAE

Scholar of Brasenose College, Oxford, 1952–1956.

B.A. First Class Honours in Literae Humaniores (Philosophy and Ancient History) 1956; M.A. 1959.

John Locke Scholar, Oxford University, 1956.

Harmsworth Senior Scholar, Merton College, Oxford, 1957.

Bachelor of Philosophy, Oxford, 1958.

Lecturer, Christ Church and Magdalen College, Oxford, 1959–1961.

Fellow and Tutor, Brasenose College, Oxford, and University Lecturer in Philosophy, 1961–1993.

*Visiting Appointments*

Visiting Professor, University of Minnesota, Fall Quarter 1963 and Spring Quarter 1985.

Visiting Professor, Cornell University, Fall Semester 1968.

Fellow of National Humanities Center, North Carolina, 1990–1991.

*Other Appointments*

Radcliffe Fellowship in Philosophy, 1973–1975.

Vice-Principal, Brasenose College, Oxford, 1987–1990.

Director of Graduate Studies in Philosophy, Oxford University, 1988–1990.

General Editor, Clarendon Plato Series, Oxford University Press.

## Michael Woods's Published Writings

*Books*

*Aristotle, Eudemian Ethics, Books One, Two, and Eight,* translated with a Commentary and Notes. (Clarendon Aristotle Series.) Oxford: Clarendon Press, 1982, 2nd edn. 1992.
*Four Prague Lectures and Other Texts,* ed. P. Rezek. Rezek: Prague, 1997.

*Articles*

'The Individuation of Things and Places', *Proceedings of the Aristotelian Society, Supplementary Volume,* 37 (1963).

'Identity and Individuation', in R. J. Butler (ed.), *Analytical Philosophy,* Second Series (Oxford: Blackwell, 1965).

'Problems in Metaphysics Z, Chapter 13', in J. M. E. Moravcsik (ed.), *Aristotle: Critical Essays* (New York: Doubleday, 1967).

'Reference and Self-Identification', *Journal of Philosophy,* 65, No. 19 (1968).

'Reasons for Action and Desires', *Proceedings of the Aristotelian Society, Supplementary Volume,* 46 (1972).

'Substance and Essence in Aristotle', *Proceedings of the Aristotelian Society,* 75 (1975).

'Existence and Tense', in Gareth Evans and John McDowell (eds.), *Truth and Meaning* (Oxford: Clarendon Press, 1976).

'Scepticism and Natural Knowledge', *Proceedings of the Aristotelian Society,* 80 (1979).

'Intuition and Perception in Aristotle's Ethics', *Oxford Studies in Ancient Philosophy,* 4 (1986).

'Plato's Division of the Soul', The Dawes Hicks Annual Philosophy Lecture, 1987, *Proceedings of the British Academy,* 1989.

'Aristotle on *Akrasia*', in A. Alberti (ed.), *Studi sull'Etica di Aristotele* (Naples, 1990).

'Universal and Particular Forms in Aristotle's *Metaphysics*',

*Oxford Studies in Ancient Philosophy*, Supplement 1991. This also appeared in H. Blumenthal and H. Robinson (eds.), *Aristotle and the Later Tradition* (Oxford: Clarendon Press, 1991).

'Particular Forms Revisited', *Phronesis*, 36 (1991).

'Aristotle on Sleep and Dreams', *Apeiron*, 25 (1992).

'Aristotle's Anthropocentrism', *Philosophical Investigations*, 16 (1993).

'Form, Species, and Predication in Aristotle', *Synthese*, 96 (1993).

'The Essence of a Human Being and the Individual Soul in Metaphysics Z and H', in T. Scaltsas, D. Charles, and M. C. Gill (eds.), *Unity, Identity, and Explanation in Aristotle's Metaphysics* (Oxford: Clarendon Press, 1994).

# INDEX

counter-intuitive ascriptions of truth-
value to conditionals 14
counterfactual dependence 52
Counterfactuality Thesis 40, 78, 90 n.
'counterfactuals' 4–8, 15, 28, 40,
    95–100, 127–36
  and possible worlds 40–57, 118–20
  and 'subjunctive' 5, 7, 40, 95, 97 n.,
    98, 112
  logical form 78–92, 111
  with impossible antecedents 45, 47,
    57, 92, 112, 135–6
  with true antecedents 45–6, 112–13
  *see also* backtracking conditionals

Davidson, Donald 97, 104
Davis, Wayne A. 53–4
deduction of consequent from
  antecedent 106
degree of belief, *see* belief, degree of
Descartes, René 112
desires, *see* conditional desires
disjunction 25, 27, 121–2, 132–3
  and assertibility 34–6, 103
  and conditional commands 125
  in antecedent 27–8, 62–4, 121–2
  in consequent 122
dispositions 83, 88–91, 96
Downing, P. B. 50, 118
Dudman, V. H. 5 n., 9 n., 15, 73 n.,
    78–9 nn., 82–3 n., 89 n., 97–8,
    100, 127–9, 131
Dummett, Michael 14 n., 60–1, 65,
    75 n., 102–3, 123, 125–6

Edgington, Dorothy 11–12 n., 31,
    69–72, 118 n.
Ellis, Brian 127
embedded conditionals, *see* compound
  conditionals
entailment and implication of falsehood of antecedent 5
epistemic state 16–17, 28, 32, 54, 59,
    69, 72, 112–13, 131–2, 135
  ideal epistemic perspective 83–6,
    91–2, 134
'even if' 127

falsity of antecedent 20–1, 29, 64–5, 99
  and conditional probability 24, 28,
    38
  *see also* 'counterfactuals'
fears, *see* conditional fears

forward-looking conditionals 86, 91–2,
    133–5; *see also* 'will' and 'would'
Frege, Gottlob 58, 95, 97
future tense, *see* tense of verb

Gibbard, Allan 15, 28, 32, 65, 66 n.,
    72–3 n., 118 n., 123
Goodman, Nelson 15, 55–6
Grice, H. P. 12–13, 17, 33–6, 38–9, 60,
    67 n., 102–3, 104–5
grounds for assertion or belief 12,
    16–17, 25, 74, 83, 102; *see also*
  connection between antecedent
  and consequent

Hare, R. M. 19 n.
hypothetical adding of antecedent to
  one's stock of knowledge 17–18,
    20, 56; *see also* Ramsey's Test

ideal epistemic perspective, *see* epistemic state
'if', *see* meaning, of 'if'
impossible antecedents, *see* 'counterfactuals', with impossible antecedents
'indicative' conditionals 9–10, 95–6; *see
  also* 'subjunctive'
inference to the best explanation
    99–100, 136
iterated conditionals, *see* compound
  conditionals

Jackson, Frank 12 n., 13–14, 19–20,
    36–7, 54 n., 58–62, 64, 85 n.,
    102–3 nn., 113, 120, 123, 125

knowledge, speaker's state of, *see* epistemic state

laws of nature 49–52, 55–6, 91, 134
Lewis, David 7 n., 13–14, 31–2, 40,
    43–52, 54–5, 57–60, 66, 102–3 nn.,
    111, 114, 117–19, 121, 124
Limit Assumption 45–6

McGee, Vann 121 n.
McKay, Thomas 122
Mackie, J. L. 6–7 nn., 15-16, 19 n.,
    66 n.
material conditionals 12–19, 31, 33, 37,
    58–9, 69–70, 101–2; *see also* Simple
  Conditionals, and truth-condi-
  tions of material conditionals

*Index*